The Instant Guide to Healthy
Succulents

Series editor: David Longman

The Instant Guide to Healthy
Succulents

John Pilbeam

Times
BOOKS

THE AUTHOR

John Pilbeam has grown, studied and written about cacti and
succulents for over thirty years. He is Secretary of the
Mammillaria Society, a qualified judge of the British
Cactus and Succulent Society and a member of the International
Organization for Succulent Plant Study.

Originally published in Great Britain in 1984 as *How to Care for
Your Succulents* by Peter Lowe, London.

Library of Congress Catalog Card Number: 84-40635
International Standard Book Number: 0-8129-1175-X

Printed in Italy by Amilcare Pizzi SpA

987654321
First American Edition

Contents

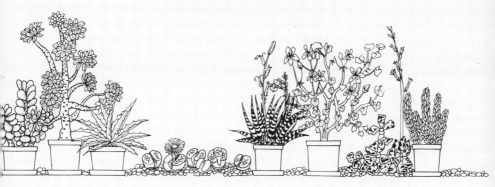

Scientific names

Introduction

How to use this book

Succulents are interesting and unusual plants to grow in the home. As a group they come from dry regions where there is little rainfall and have become specially adapted to desert or near desert conditions. Stem succulents store water in thickened stems or underground tubers and produce new leaves every year only to lose them in the dry period. Leaf succulents have thick wax-coated leaves which shrink and shrivel but do not dry out completely. They vary in shape and size from inch-high pebble-like plants to full-sized trees, though indoors very few will grow inconveniently large.

Cacti are also succulent plants and are covered in another book in this series, 'How to care for your Cacti'. The main difference between cacti and all other succulent plants is that cactus spines grow from a felty pad or areole.

Succulents need rather different care from most other indoor plants and will not grow well in the wrong conditions. This book is here to help you to succeed.

Each two-page spread is devoted to one type of plant. The left-hand page describes the plant, explaining how to look after it and the correct amount of water, light or feeding it requires. There is also a colour photo of a healthy plant. On the right hand page is a colour painting showing all the things that can go wrong. Since this picture shows all the problems at once, some of the plants look very sick indeed! To find out what is wrong with your plant, look for its symptoms on the illustration. Read the caption next to the part of the picture which shows the same features as your plant. It tells you what is wrong and how to put it right.

Succulents are tough plants, and will stand quite a lot of neglect but with correct care they will develop their full potential and produce their striking flowers.

Tools for indoor gardening
Succulents can be cared for with very little special equipment and you can acquire what you need gradually as your collection grows.

Keep separate sprayers and watering cans for insecticides and fungicides. Methylated spirits is useful for removing some pests. Mark all containers clearly and wash them out regularly. Buy only small quantities.

A sharp knife is used for cuttings and paring away damaged roots and stems. Scissors and secateurs are useful.

Seed trays or half-pots are needed for propagation. Small square pots are sometimes available for single plants. A thermometer is useful, especially in a greenhouse.

A small garden trowel is useful when mixing compost, repotting or adding topsoil to large plants. A large spoon is a good substitute. A plastic bowl or deep tray is essential for mixing composts.

Keep a selection of loam-based or peat-based composts, coarse gritty sand and gravel for top-dressing. Special sand can be obtained from garden centres. Fertilizer and hormone rooting powder containing fungicide are useful.

A watering can with a narrow spout is useful for watering into small pots. Never use your normal watering can for insecticides or fungicides.

Gloves are essential for handling spiny plants such as Agaves. A paintbrush is useful for removing pests and cotton wool buds help to remove them from crevices.

Keep a small stock of pots, half-pots and saucers, both plastic and clay. Outer pots with no drainage holes can be used to hide standard pots but never let water stand inside them.

Clingfilm or polythene bags can be used to cover seedlings to retain moisture. A few succulents may need training with twine.

Scientific names

Few succulent plants have popular names and these vary from place to place. The plants in this book are all identified under their full scientific names. All plants (and animals) are classified into groups known as families which are subdivided into genera (singular genus) and then again into species and perhaps varieties. Plants in the same genus but of different species share some basic characteristics but may look very different in size, shape or colouring (the flower is the most obvious constant factor). A variety is only slightly different from another variety of the same species. Hybrids are crosses between two different species or sometimes even genera. Correctly labelled plants have a genus name followed by the species and, if appropriate, the variety. For hybrids the second part of the name is put in inverted commas and is usually more popular than scientific, e.g. *Crassula* 'Morgan's Beauty'.

Light and temperature

The most important factor in caring for succulent plants is light. Their healthy growth, the development of their colouring and flowers are directly related to the amount of light you allow them. Ideally the all-round light of a sun-bathed greenhouse is what they need, but an uncurtained sunny windowsill will do very well for most. In winter months, when light levels are lower, it is more important still to ensure that they remain in the lightest position possible. If indoors, keep them on the windowsill, only removing them at night if you close the curtains; otherwise in cold climates they may be damaged in the ice-box created between the curtains and the window on frosty nights. Try not to keep them too hot in winter or their natural growing cycle will be disturbed. Around 50°F (10°C) is ideal. If in a greenhouse a minimum temperature of 40°F (4°C), or better, 45°F (7°C), should be maintained in winter.

If a greenhouse is very exposed to summer sunshine, it may be necessary to

Succulent families

Many of the succulent plants in this book are specially adapted members of families which also include well-known wild or garden plants.

Agavaceae: Century plant family 1
Agave

Apocynaceae: Periwinkle family 2
Adenium, Pachypodium

Asclepiadaceae: Carrion flower family 3
Caralluma, Ceropegia, Duvalia, Huernia, Orbea, Stapelia

Compositae: Groundsel family 4
Senecio

Crassulaceae: Stonecrop family 5
Adromischus, Aeonium, Cotyledon, Crassula, Dudleya, Echeveria, Graptopetalum, Kalanchoe, Pachyphytum, Sedum

Dioscoreaceae: Bryony family 6
Testudinaria

Euphorbiaceae: Spurge family 7
Euphorbia

Geraniaceae: Geranium family 8
Pelargonium

Liliaceae: Lily family 9
Aloe, Gasteria, Haworthia

Mesembryanthemaceae: Midday flower family 10
Conophytum, Faucaria, Fenestraria, Gibbaeum, Lithops, Pleiospilos

Portulacaceae: Purslane family 11
Portulacaria

Watering

1. Test compost for dryness with knife blade or plant label before watering. If blade comes out clean, soil is dry. If soil sticks, it is still moist. Check instructions for each plant before watering.

2. Add water to top of pot, filling it to brim. Excess will drain into saucer. After ½ an hour, empty away any left in saucer. Never leave pot standing in water.

3. If plant has leaves that will be marked by water, fill saucer under pot with water. Wait for ½ an hour, then empty away what is left.

the most frequent cause of failure. Most need a winter rest in the 2 or 3 coldest months, sparse watering in spring and autumn, and more frequent watering in the summer months. But some differ, so check the plant's entry to find its particular requirements; it is a good idea to put the basic needs on a label in the pot so that you are reminded as you care for your plants of when and when not to water.

When you do water them at whatever time of year, do so generously. Quickly fill the space between the top of the compost and the rim of the pot and allow the water to drain into the soil. If any is left standing in the saucer after about ½ an hour, be sure to drain it off. Do not water again until the soil has nearly dried out from the previous watering. This can be tested by inserting a thin plant label or the blade of a knife into the soil: if it comes out moist, leave for a few more days, and test again. If in doubt do not water.

Feeding

Provided that they are repotted each year most succulent plants do not really need feeding, but some benefit from it and instructions for feeding these plants are given with each entry. Always use a fertilizer with a high potash content, like those used for tomatoes, roses or chrysanthemums. Liquid types are probably the easiest to use. Use them at the strength recommended for use on potted plants. Always dilute them or the plant will be damaged. If a plant which does not normally need feeding fails to grow well, the compost may be too poor. If you notice this in spring or in early to midsummer, repot in a different compost straight away. If later in the year, feed the plant until watering is reduced, then repot the following spring. Some fertilizers leave unsightly stains on plants if they are poured over the top of them so it is best to water them straight on to the top of the compost. If when watering some drops do fall on the leaves, do not brush them off but blow gently to disperse the droplets.

shade the glass at times to prevent scorching. Succulent plants seem particularly vulnerable to this in the spring, when the sun suddenly shines strongly after weeks of cloudy weather and the plants are a little on the soft side, especially if they have recently been watered.

Watering

In the wild succulent plants usually receive water at certain times of the year only, and then often in quantity, with flash floods washing over them, or even submerging them for hours at a time. However, the water drains away quickly and the plants must be able to take it up rapidly and store it for long periods of drought. This is made possible by their structure, which allows the stems or leaves to swell in times of plenty, and then store water during dry periods, releasing little by way of evaporation. Succulents grown indoors need the same annual dry period and ignoring it is

9

Repotting

1–2 weeks before repotting, water soil so that root ball will come from the pot easily.

1. Hold plant gently round base of stem, with gloves on if plant is spiny. Tap pot rim against edge of table or bench and gently ease root ball out onto a clear space. Check roots for root mealy bug and growth.

2. Prepare new pot with layer of compost deep enough to plant root ball at same level as before, about 1in (2½cm) below rim of pot. If soil falls away easily, shake off old compost. If not, do not disturb root ball.

3. Place plant in centre of new pot. Be careful not to damage any mealy covering on leaves. Trickle new compost around root ball to fill pot.

4. Firm compost lightly around stem but do not press down too hard.

5. Add a final layer of grit to top of compost. Do not water for 2 weeks after repotting.

Choosing the compost

Succulent plants need a well-drained, nutritious mixture, which will allow good root development, and supply water without staying too soggy for too long.

Loam-based compost is made up of sterilized loam (soil) mixed with peat and grit or coarse, washed sand. It is usually sold with fertilizer added, following formulae developed by the John Innes Institute for Horticultural Research. The numbers 1, 2 and 3 indicate the different proportions of fertilizer added (No. 3 is the strongest). In this book they are referred to as 'loam-based compost No. 1, 2 or 3'.

Either loam-based or peat-based composts can be used neat, but to encourage the more rapid drying-out succulents need, they are best mixed with 1 part coarse, gritty sand to 2 parts of compost. On no account use builders' or seashore sand, which will not be sterile and may have a high lime or salt content.

Repotting

Plastic pots have almost entirely superseded clay ones for succulent plant cultivation, although for some, such as Lithops, Conophytum or Pleiospilos, clay has advantages, allowing moisture to evaporate very quickly so that the compost is never moist for more than a few days.

The best time for repotting is in late winter to early spring, before fresh roots have started to develop. Check the condition of the plant's roots when removing from the pot. If the root-ball is solid and there are plenty of new roots, repot it in a pot one size larger than the old one. If the compost falls away easily, but there is a good root system, the plant can be repotted in the same sized pot with fresh compost. This applies also to plants that are nearly full grown and are in pots of 5in (13cm) or more. If using the same pot, wash it out well and dry it before replanting.

Many succulent plants are shallow rooted and will do better in half-pots or pans shallower than their width. For plants with thick, tuberous roots use a pot deep enough to contain the roots without cramping them.

Always place the plant at the same level as it was before and add a final top layer of grit to the compost. This prevents the compost becoming compacted into a hard layer after watering, stops the water washing up around the plant and marking the leaves with a 'tide-mark' and helps prevent too rapid drying out in hot weather.

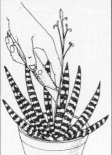

After flowering
When flowers die, cut stem with sharp scissors or secateurs close to base. Or wait until it pulls out easily by hand. Do not force out or plant may be damaged.

Treating damaged roots
1. Remove plant from pot and check for root rot if no healthy new growth appears in spring. If root is black and soft, pare away thinly from the base with a very sharp knife until no speck of black remains. If any left, rot will return.

2. Dust with hormone rooting powder containing fungicide to prevent further infection and leave to dry for 2–3 days before repotting in dry compost. Leave dry for 2–3 weeks, until new roots form.

3. Plants with fibrous roots can be treated in the same way, though the roots themselves will have disappeared and the stem must be cut away until only healthy tissue remains.

Cleaning

Many succulent plants have a waxy bloom which will be damaged by spraying. They are best kept free from dust by occasionally blowing: short sharp puffs close to the dusty part will usually clean them efficiently. Never use leafshine.

Propagation

Many succulent plants are very easily propagated from cuttings of either whole shoots or in many cases of just individual leaves. Those difficult to propagate in this way can usually be grown from seed, obtainable from specialist nurseries.

Cuttings: The best time to take cuttings of most plants is in late spring or early summer, when the plant is growing vigorously. Do not do it while the plant is actually producing flowers. The basic method of taking cuttings is illustrated on p.12. Remember that cuttings must never be placed straight into fresh soil and watered – the cut surface must be allowed to dry and harden to prevent harmful fungi invading the tissue; the larger the cut surface the longer they need to be left to dry. It is a good idea to dust all cut surfaces with hormone rooting powder containing fungicide since this is the most convenient way of preventing infection.

Some succulent plants will produce a new plant from a detached, rooted leaf. Gently ease off a whole leaf from where it joins the stem. After allowing the end to dry out for a few days in an empty pot, place it on top of dry compost. Some can be laid flat, others end down. The important thing is that they are in close contact with the compost all the time. The leaf will shortly form roots, and a small plant will grow from its base.

Seeds: Succulent plant seeds need warmth and moisture to encourage germination just like those of other plants, and seedlings that survive in the wild do so usually because they have found a niche where they are protected from the drying effect of the hot sun until they are large enough to withstand it. Sowing is best carried out in a place where light and temperature can be carefully controlled. They do not need very high temperatures so a heated propagator is not essential. The seedlings in their first few weeks or even months must be kept from drying out by a covering of polythene or cling film.

Grafting: Some succulents are difficult to grow on their own roots, and are sold grafted on to more easily grown plants, from which they draw their nourishment.

Taking cuttings

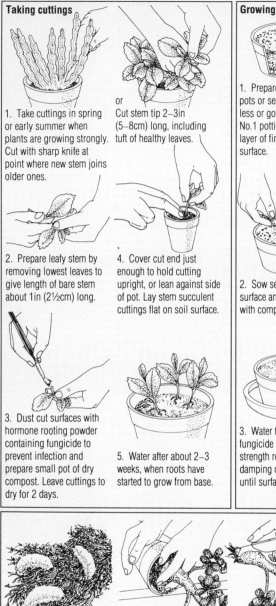

1. Take cuttings in spring or early summer when plants are growing strongly. Cut with sharp knife at point where new stem joins older ones.

or
Cut stem tip 2–3in (5–8cm) long, including tuft of healthy leaves.

2. Prepare leafy stem by removing lowest leaves to give length of bare stem about 1in (2½cm) long.

3. Dust cut surfaces with hormone rooting powder containing fungicide to prevent infection and prepare small pot of dry compost. Leave cuttings to dry for 2 days.

4. Cover cut end just enough to hold cutting upright, or lean against side of pot. Lay stem succulent cuttings flat on soil surface.

5. Water after about 2–3 weeks, when roots have started to grow from base.

Growing from seed

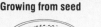

1. Prepare 3½in (9cm) half pots or seed trays with soil-less or good loam based No.1 potting compost and a layer of fine grit on the surface.

2. Sow seed thinly on the surface and do not cover with compost.

3. Water from below with fungicide diluted to strength recommended for damping off of seedlings until surface looks moist.

4. Place pots or tray in polythene bag, sealing ends underneath to prevent moisture escaping. Or, seal with clingfilm.

5. Keep at 70°F (21°C) in light place, not direct sunlight, for 6 months or more, until seedlings are the size of a small garden pea. Do not water unless moisture film on polythene becomes patchy or dries out.

6. Prick out seedlings into new trays or small pots, planting about 1in (2½cm) apart.

Vine weevils

Drastic treatment is needed to cure vine weevil attack. Vine weevils lay eggs on soil and larvae invade roots and stem. Adult flies are rarely seen by day.

1. If stem is swollen and round pieces chewed from leaves, remove from pot and inspect roots.

2. Starting at base of plant, pare away thin slices of root, then stem until soft area with larvae is reached. Cut away completely until no sign of larvae or rot remains.

3. Dust with hormone rooting powder and leave dry for 2–3 days before repotting in clean pot in new compost. Do not water for 2–3 weeks, when new roots will have formed.

Grafting succulents is really a job for experts but remember that the grafted plant you purchase is really two plants. It should be watered according to the needs of the lower part but as far as temperature is concerned follow instructions for the upper part. When buying a grafted plant always try to find out what the rootstock (the lower part) is so that you do not give the wrong care.

Pests and insecticides

When pests attack they are often very difficult to eradicate completely, and the damage they cause may be irreparable. It is better to prevent attack rather than wait to treat the results.

Carry out a regular programme of treatment with insecticides, once a month in the growing season and once or twice when the plants are dormant. In the growing period you can use both contact and systemic insecticides, except on those plants which are susceptible to damage from them.

Contact insecticides are sprayed on to the plants and kill the pests when they make contact with them; systemic insecticides are either sprayed or watered into the soil and work both by contact and by entering the plant's system so that any sap-sucking insect takes in the poison as it feeds. In winter use only contact sprays, in dry weather, so that the plant does not stay wet for too long.

Some pests, such as root mealy bug, are almost impossible to detect just by looking at the plant and are only discovered when repotting. Always inspect the roots carefully to make sure they are healthy before potting in fresh compost.

Insecticides are dangerous to humans and animals as well as to plants. Spray plants outside in the early morning on a fine, still day, out of direct sunlight. Leave them out for several hours. In a greenhouse, work from the far end towards the door. Keep out until the vapour has dispersed.

Taking care with insecticides

Insecticides and fungicides may contain deadly chemicals. Use them with care.

Never mix different types of insecticides as the chemicals may react.

Never put them into other bottles, such as soft drink or beer bottles.

Never breathe in the spray.

Never spray in windy weather.

Never pour them down the sink or drains. Do not even pour the water in which you have washed containers and sprayers down the drain.

Never make up more at one time than you will use.

Never keep diluted insecticide for more than 24 hours.

Never leave old containers lying around.

Never stay in a greenhouse after spraying.

Always follow instructions carefully. Do not over or under dilute.

Always use a separate watering can and sprayer, keeping another one for normal spraying and watering.

Always keep away from food, crockery, glasses, food containers, and minerals. Derris is harmful to fish; malathion harms bees.

Always cover fish bowls when spraying.

Always store them with their sprayers and containers in a dry, frost free place, on a high shelf out of reach of children.

Always spray outside, when bees are not around. Early morning best.

Always wash out all sprayers and empty bottles after use, inside and out.

Always pour washing water onto ground away from food crops and water sources such as streams and rivers.

Always throw empty bottles and containers away with domestic waste.

Always wash thoroughly in hot water and detergent when you have used them.

Adenium obesum

This attractive plant is popularly known as the Desert Rose as when in full bloom it looks like a rose bush covered in flowers. The thick stem, with its bulbous base, sits just above the soil and from this other more slender stems branch out. The flowers appear before the leaves, in late spring, when the plant starts to come out of its winter rest period. After flowering, the thick, waxy leaves appear and the plant grows throughout the summer. *Adenium obesum* is the species most commonly seen and is available either as seed or as seedling plants. These grow after 3–4 years to a foot (30cm) tall if repotted regularly and watered in summer. Others occasionally available are *A. swazicum* and *A. oleifolium*.

Adenium obesum, the Desert rose, has a thick swollen stem called a caudex which in the wild stores water and enables the plant to survive severe drought. The swollen part should be planted above the soil for if it is allowed to stay damp underground, it may rot.

Light: Full sunlight is essential for growth and to encourage flower production.

Temperature: Minimum 50°F (10°C) is needed. Give fresh air in summer, or stand outside when all danger of frost is past.

Water: Start watering every 2 weeks in late spring, allowing to dry out between waterings. Water weekly in hottest months, then fortnightly again in autumn. Leave dry in winter and early spring and allow plant to rest, when leaves will drop naturally. See also Introduction.

Feeding: Use high potash fertilizer in summer once a month, stop in autumn.

Soil: Use good loam-based No. 2 potting compost, or soil-less compost, with about 40% gritty sand to improve drainage.

Repotting: Every year when young and growing quickly but when over 6in (15cm) tall, better to change top inch (2½cm) soil with fresh and feed regularly as root disturbance causes the roots to rot off.

Propagation: Only possible from seeds, available from specialist nurseries.

Leaves blacken and fall, stem ends soft, tuber soft. Too cold and wet. Move to warmer place, at least 55°F (13°C) and allow to dry out before watering again. Always keep dry in winter even in normal room temperatures. Pare away rotting tissue and dust with fungicide. If conditions correct, check roots for sciara fly or vine weevil maggots (see Introduction). If rot is severe, plant will die.

Trimming dead shoots
In winter stem tips may shrivel and die if not sprayed. Wait until they are quite dry before cutting off with sharp scissors or secateurs. Cut just inside dry area to avoid damaging healthy tissue.

White woolly patches among leaves. Mealy bug. Remove with small paintbrush dipped in methylated spirits, and spray with insecticide. Repeat 2 or 3 times in growing season.

Flowers shrivel quickly. Too hot and dry. Check soil regularly in summer and water when it dries out. Do not expose to hot sun after cloudy weather: move gradually into full light.

what goes wrong

Little sign of new growth in spring. Needs feeding or repotting or root mealy bug. Check roots and if white woolly patches found, wash soil away, swirl roots in insecticide and allow to dry before repotting.

Leaves turn pale, shrivel and fall. In summer, too hot and dry or too wet. Check conditions. If dry, soak in bowl of water for ½ an hour, then drain. If soil dark and soggy, leave to dry out completely before watering again. If new leaves do not grow but stem firm, repot in fresh, dry compost. Do not water again for 2 weeks. Leaves fall naturally in autumn/winter and grow again in spring.

Tips of shoots die back, becoming brown and hard; shoots break out from well below tips in spring. Spraying tips in winter will stop this excessive drying up. Remove damaged tips when absolutely dry with sharp scissors.

Leaves turn pale green or yellow-green, no flowers. Too dark. Bring gradually into full sun over 2 weeks.

Leaves marked with brown or white patches. Brown is scorch from sudden hot sun in stuffy place. White is from insecticides or hard water spray. Remove with rainwater and small paintbrush.

When received plant has soft patches in bulbous stem or roots, and on cutting, orange patches in the tissue are revealed. Damage to roots has allowed orange rot to get a hold. Pare away narrow slices with sharp clean knife until no sign of orange is visible. Dust with hormone rooting powder containing fungicide; allow to dry thoroughly before rerooting in dry compost.

15

Adromischus cooperi

No more than five species of this small, beautifully spotted genus are widely known in cultivation though others can be found at specialist nurseries. They come from South Africa, and make good indoor or greenhouse plants, provided they get enough sun to bring out their colouring. *Adromischus cooperi* grows to about 2in (5cm) high and spreads 4–6in (10–15cm) across. It has thick roots, like underground stems or rhizomes and these are best kept with the top just above the surface of the compost, to avoid any risk of rotting. The other species usually grown are: *Adromischus trigynus* (often named *A. maculatus*), *A. marianae*, *A. mammillaris* and *A. triebneri*. Do not use insecticides such as malathion or any labelled as unsuitable for Crassulas or Crassulaceae. Pyrethrum-based types are safe.

Adromischus cooperi, also known as the Plover's egg plant from the attractive mottling on its leaves, will not usually outgrow a 5 or 6in (15cm) pan. It needs very good light to keep the colouring of its leaves and if cared for correctly will produce its long spike of flowers in late summer. New plants are easy to propagate from single leaves.

Light: Maximum sunlight is needed for best colouring and to keep them compact.
Temperature: A minimum of 40°F (4°C). Give fresh air in summer and if in a greenhouse, keep under 100°F (37°C).
Water: Start watering fortnightly in spring. Leave to dry out between waterings. Water weekly in hot weather, then fortnightly again in the autumn. Leave dry in winter. See also Introduction.
Feeding: Not necessary but if not repotted, feed once or twice in summer with high potash fertilizer.
Soil: Use good loam-based No. 2 potting compost, or soil-less compost, with about 40% coarse gritty sand to improve drainage.
Repotting: Every spring in size larger half-pot or pan, being careful not to dislodge weakly attached leaves. Keep top of thick roots just above soil to prevent rotting.
Propagation: From leaves.

No new growth. Needs feeding. Feed twice in summer with high potash fertilizer. If fed regularly, check roots for root mealy bug. If white woolly patches on roots, swirl in pyrethrum-based insecticide and allow to dry before repotting in fresh compost and clean pot. Leave dry for 2 weeks.

Propagation

1. In late spring when new leaves appear, gently remove 3 or 4 from near top. Leave in safe place such as in empty pot to dry for 2 days.

2. Place on pot of dry compost with end touching surface; do not insert into compost but lean against pot rim or hold in place with soil. Do not water until new roots show. A new plantlet will grow from base of leaf but do not remove old leaf until quite dead and dry.

Green or black insects on flower stalk. Greenfly or blackfly. Spray with pyrethrum-based insecticide, protecting leaves with paper. Repeat every 10 days until clear.

After flowering
When flowers die, cut stem with sharp scissors or secateurs close to base. Or wait until it pulls out easily by hand. Do not force out or plant may be damaged.

Leaves pale, stems tall with spaces between leaves. No flowers. Too dark or too hot in winter. Move into good light and keep below 50°F (10°C) in winter.

Leaves distorted. Insecticide damage. Use only pyrethrum-based insecticides. Not usually fatal.

Leaves dry up and drop in summer. If stem firm, too dry. Soak pot in bowl of water for ½ hour, then drain and water more regularly. If all leaves fall, much too dry or too wet. Check conditions. Allow to dry out if soggy and check drainage and compost mix. Some shrivelling natural in winter.

Leaves turn black and fall. Stem soft. Too cold, wet and humid. Keep dry in winter, above 40°F (4°C). If conditions correct, check roots for sciara fly or vine weevil maggots. If stem rotted but leaves healthy, start new plants from leaf cuttings.

what goes wrong

White woolly patches on leaves. Mealy bug. Remove with small paintbrush dipped in methylated spirits, and spray with pyrethrum-based insecticide. Repeat 2 or 3 times in growing season.

Leaves dry with brown patches. Sun scorch, exposed too quickly to strong sun, with poor ventilation. Move out of sun, then move back gradually over 2 weeks. Keep in more airy place.

17

Aeonium arboreum

The variety of *Aeonium arboreum* shown here, *Aeonium arboreum var atropurpureum*, has a topknot of blackish-purple leaves at the end of each spongy stem. It comes from the Canary Islands and needs very bright sunlight to bring out the purple colouring of its leaves. It will grow up to 1½–2ft (50–60cm) tall and 6–12in (20–30cm) across. It is important not to use spray insecticides labelled as unsuitable for Crassulas or Crassulacae as they will distort leaves and kill the plant. Those based on pyrethrum are safe. Other species include *A. decorum* and *A. haworthii*, like bonsai trees; *A. tabulaeforme*, with low, flat rosettes; and *A. sedifolium* with tiny rounded leaves.

Aeonium arboreum var atropurpureum is one of the darkest leaved succulent plants and may look almost black if kept in a sunny spot. Like most Aeoniums it tends to get large and straggly after a few years and it is best to start again with cuttings, which root easily. It is not easy to flower indoors.

Light: To keep the purple colouring the sunniest spot you can provide is essential, otherwise the plant becomes green and grows out of shape. Put outside in summer to increase chances of flowering.

Temperature: A minimum of 40°F (4°C) is needed; stand outside in summer and over 2 weeks gradually move into full sunlight.

Water: Start watering every 2 weeks in spring, increasing to once a week in summer but always allowing soil to dry out between waterings. Reduce gradually again in autumn and in winter water only once a month if leaves start to shrivel. See also Introduction.

Feeding: Use high potash fertilizer in summer only, once a month.

Soil: Use good loam-based No. 2 potting compost, or soil-less compost, with 30% coarse, gritty sand for improved drainage.

Propagation: Take cuttings 2–3in (8cm) long from young shoots which grow on main stem.

Taking cuttings

1. In spring or early summer cut 2–3in (5–8cm) long shoot from main stem with sharp knife. Choose healthy stem with good head of leaves.

2. Dust cut surfaces with hormone rooting powder to prevent infection. Allow cutting to dry for 2 days, then place on dry compost in small pot. Do not water until roots appear.

what goes wrong

Leaves small and few. Too dry or needs repotting. Check conditions. If bone dry, soak for ½ an hour in bowl of water, drain, then water more regularly except in winter. If watering correct, plant outgrowing pot. Repot in spring in next size pot.

Small green insects on and between leaves. Greenfly. Spray with pyrethrum-based insecticide and repeat every 10 days until clear.

Plant thin and straggly, rosettes lose colour. Too hot and wet in winter. Keep in dry, airy place, not more than 50°F (10°C).

Leaves turn black and fall, stem ends black and soft. Too cold and wet, overwatered. Move to warmer place, over 40°F (4°C) in winter. Pare away blackened stem and dust with fungicide. Keep dry in winter. At other times always allow soil to dry out before watering.

Leaves scorched. Too much sun too quickly. Move out of direct sun, reintroduce gradually over 2 weeks. Keep in more airy place.

Leaves shrivel and fall in winter. Too dry. Add just enough water to moisten soil once a month.

White woolly patches on leaves and stem, especially on young shoots. Mealy bug. Remove with paintbrush dipped in methylated spirits and spray with pyrethrum-based insecticide. Repeat after 10 days if not clear.

Leaves turn plain green. Too dark. Move over 2 weeks into strong sunlight.

Leaves droop. Too dry or root damage from pests or overwatering. If dry, soak in bowl of water for half an hour, drain and give more water in future. If wet, dry out, remove from pot and treat roots if rotted or infected (see Introduction).

Round pieces missing from leaf edges, stem swollen, no growth. Vine weevil. Dust around base with insecticide powder and pare away stem until larvae removed.

Little growth, white woolly patches on roots. Root mealy bug. Wash roots and swirl in insecticide. Dry for 2–3 days, then repot in fresh compost and clean soil. Leave dry for 2 weeks.

Agave utahensis

This plant is from the desert areas of Utah and Nevada in the USA and is one of the smaller growing Agave species suitable for indoor culture, growing to between 6 and 8in (15–20cm) tall and 8–10in (20–25cm) across. Most Agaves are large plants, some up to 10ft (3m) tall and wide. The leaves are very stiff and very sharply pointed. The flowers, which will not appear for 10 or 20 years, are not welcome as the plant dies after flowering. They are known as 'Century plants' as it was believed they flowered only once in 100 years. Other species worth growing are *A. parviflora*, *A. filifera*, *A. victoria-reginae*, and *A. americana*, a larger one.

Light: As much sun as possible to keep their shape and colour.

Temperature: A minimum of 40°F (4°C) is needed for safety, although most Agaves will take quite low temperatures if dry, even a little below freezing.

Water: Start to water in spring and allow to dry out between waterings. About once a fortnight is enough in spring and summer. Leave completely dry in winter. See also Introduction.

Feeding: Use high potash fertilizer in summer once a month, stop in autumn.

Soil: Use good loam-based No. 2 potting compost, or soil-less compost, with 30% gritty sand to improve drainage.

Repotting: Every spring in size larger pot, until 7 or 8in (18–20cm) pot is reached, when soil may be shaken off and plant repotted in fresh soil in the same sized pot.

Propagation: Occasionally suckering offsets are produced, which may be removed but leaves do not root to form new plants. Agaves can also be raised from seed, but buy named species; mixtures will usually be of the bigger plants.

Agave utahensis var. nevadensis. This spiky plant is grown for its leaves since the flowers do not appear for at least 10 years and the plants die after flowering. All Agaves are spiky plants and should be handled with care and kept safely out of children's reach. It is possible to receive a bad eye injury from the stiff, needle-sharp points on the leaves.

Leaf tips brown, rest light brown. Too dry or sunscorch. Check soil. If very dry, plunge into bowl of water, for 10–15 minutes, then drain. Water regularly in summer. If sunscorched, cover with paper to filter sun for 2 weeks. Cut off damaged leaves.

Leaf end hangs down, brown crack across leaf. Plant knocked or pushed against window. Cut off cleanly at break with sharp scissors; do not pull off or base of leaf may be damaged.

Leaves dry and brown. If only lowest leaves, natural. Cut off with sharp scissors. If upper leaves also brown, overwatered, centre rotting: if leaves pull out easily, too late to save plant.

what goes wrong

Plant does not grow. Needs repotting and feeding. Repot each year in fresh compost and feed monthly in summer with high potash fertilizer.

Removing offsets
Wear gloves to remove offsets in spring or early summer, cutting with sharp knife as close to main stem as possible. Dust cut surfaces with hormone rooting powder and leave offset to dry for 2 days before potting in dry compost.

Leaves long and pale. Too dark or too wet. Check conditions. Move to lighter place; allow to dry out before watering. Keep dry in winter.

Leaves black. Atmosphere too humid. Roots rotting. Plant may die but move to more airy position, in good bright light.

White woolly patches among leaves. Mealy bug. Remove with small paintbrush dipped in methylated spirits and spray with contact or systemic insecticide. Repeat 2 or 3 times in growing season.

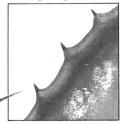

Plant doesn't grow; white woolly patches on roots. Root mealy bug. Wash soil off roots, swirl in contact insecticide, and allow to dry before repotting in fresh compost and clean pot. Leave dry for 2 weeks.

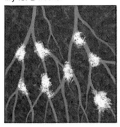

Aloe variegata

This large genus of plants from South Africa and eastern parts of Africa, varies from large trees to tiny hand-sized plants. The smaller ones are very suitable for indoor or greenhouse culture, and are primarily chosen for the markings on their leaves. The red, yellow or pink flowers appear in winter or spring; they are tube shaped and many are on a long stem like bluebells. *Aloe variegata* grows well on windowsills where it can take full advantage of the sunlight and will grow to around 12in (30cm) high. Overwatering is the commonest cause of failure. Other good species are *A. albiflora*, *A. descoingsii*, *A. haworthioides*, *A. parvula*, *A. somaliensis*.

Aloe flowers are red, yellow or pink and grow on a long stem in late winter or spring. The flowers open progressively from lower down the stem to the tip and the stem should not be removed until it has dried and withered.

Light: Maximum light is needed for best colouring and flower production.

Temperature: A minimum of 45°F (7°C) is safer for these plants, as many of them like a little water in the winter months. Give fresh air or stand outside in the summer, when no danger of frost threatens.

Water: These plants want only a little water, once a month in winter. Start watering more often in spring, building up to every week in summer, tail off again in autumn. See also Introduction.

Feeding: Use a high potash fertilizer in summer once a month, stop feeding in autumn.

Soil: Use good loam-based No. 2 potting compost, or soil-less compost, with about 30% coarse, gritty sand to improve drainage.

Repotting: Every spring in size larger pot, until in 7 or 8in (18–20cm) when soil may be shaken off and plant repotted in fresh soil in same size pot.

Propagation: From offsets which appear at soil level or low on the main stem.

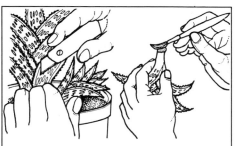

Removing offsets
1. In spring or early summer, when offsets have 3–4 pairs of leaves, remove from parent plant with sharp knife.

2. Dust cut surfaces with hormone rooting powder to prevent infection, leave to dry for 2–3 days, then plant on dry compost.

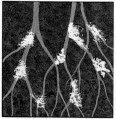

Plant does not grow, white woolly patches on roots. Root mealy bug. Wash soil off roots, swirl in contact insecticide, and allow to dry before repotting in fresh compost and clean pot. Leave dry for 2 weeks.

Green or black insects on flower stalk. Greenfly or blackfly feeding on flower's nectar. Cover leaves with paper and spray flowers with contact insecticide. Repeat weekly until clear.

what goes wrong

Leaves at centre of plant grow tall and thin, losing colour. Too hot and wet in winter; or too dark. Keep below 50°F (10°C) during dry resting period, with no water. But make sure light is good all year round.

White woolly patches among leaves. Mealy bug. Remove with small paintbrush dipped in methylated spirits, and spray with contact or systemic insecticide. Repeat 2 or 3 times in growing season.

Leaves poor colour, no flowers. Not enough light. Keep in sunniest possible place all year round.

When flowers die, cut stalk as close to base as possible. Or, wait until it pulls out easily by hand.

Black sooty covering on leaves. Sooty mould from flower nectar. Wipe off with cloth.

Most leaves turn brown and dry. Much too dry or roots lost from overwatering earlier. If dry, soak in bowl of water for ½ an hour, then drain. If no improvement, inspect and treat roots (see Introduction).

Round, brown scales on leaves. Scale insect. Spray plant and soak soil with systemic insecticide. Remove after 1 week .

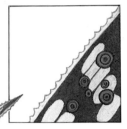

Leaves badly marked. Sun scorch. Shade with paper for 2 weeks to allow to recover.

Leaves close up or wrinkle, lower leaves brown and dry. Too dry. Test compost. If very dry, soak in bowl of water for 10–15 minutes, then drain. Water more regularly in hot weather.

Stem turns black and rots. Too cold and wet in winter, overwatered in summer. Keep dry in winter and allow to dry out between waterings during rest of year.

Caralluma frerei

Carallumas come from many desert areas and have low, angular stems, often with unpleasant-smelling flowers. *Caralluma frerei* is unusual in not having flowers with this kind of smell and also in having thick leaves growing from its sprawling stem. It grows to around 2in (5cm) tall and spreads 6–8in (15–20cm) across, comes from India, and was known for a long time as *Frerea indica*. No Carallumas should be overwatered — this is the commonest cause of loss — and they need a very sunny spot for best results, particularly for flower production. Other species seen are *Caralluma hesperidum*, with almost black flowers, *C. europaea* with brown and yellow flowers, *C. dummeri* with green flowers and *C. mammillaris* with red-brown flowers.

Caralluma carnosa's thick, green succulent stems are deeply indented and, unlike those of *Caralluma frerei* (right) do not produce leaves. The flowers are pollinated by flies and are known as carrion flowers because they are said to look (and smell) like bad meat.

Light: Full sunshine all the year round.
Temperature: A minimum of at least 50°F (10°C) in winter to prevent leaves from falling, better at 55°F (13°C). Give fresh air in summer.
Water: If at 55°F (13°C) or over in winter, water monthly, to prevent leaves falling; if lower, keep dry. Water once thoroughly in spring, and after about a month start watering once a fortnight, weekly in hottest months. Tail off in autumn. See also Introduction.
Feeding: Use a high potash fertilizer once a month in summer only.
Soil: Use good loam-based No. 2 potting compost, or soil-less compost, with about 40% coarse, gritty sand.
Repotting: Every spring into larger half-pot or pan, until 7in (18cm) is reached, when plant can be repotted in same size, or broken up and started again from cuttings.
Propagation: Grows easily from cuttings.

Plant does not grow, small black flies around plant and soil surface. Sciara or mushroom fly. Roots have probably rotted. Remove from pot and pare away stem until no trace of larvae or brown rot is left in stem tissue. Dust with hormone rooting powder and leave to dry for a few days, then lay on dry soil to reroot. If stem completely rotted and tiny white larvae with dark heads are found, dispose of plant and soil.

Leaves turn brownish black and fall off, stems soft and shrivelled. Too cold and wet. Overwatering has rotted roots. Check if still rooted by lifting stems gently off soil; they will come away in your hand if roots have rotted. Treat roots (see Introduction). In future water more carefully and keep at least 55°F (13°C) in winter.

Plant shows little sign of growth. Needs feeding. If fed regularly, check roots. White woolly patches on roots are root mealy bug. Wash all soil off roots, swirl in contact insecticide, and allow to dry before repotting. Leave dry for 2 weeks.

Taking cuttings

1. Take cuttings in spring with sharp knife, cutting off 2–3in (5–8cm) stem tip which includes 3–4 healthy leaves. Remove lowest leaf if no bare stem below it on cutting.

2. Dust base of cutting and cut end of stem with hormone rooting powder to prevent infection and leave cutting to dry for 2 days.

3. Prepare small pot and lay stem flat on surface of dry compost. Do not water until roots appear. May take 4–6 weeks.

Stems grow straggly, leaves pale at tips. No flowers in summer. Too dark. Needs full light all the year round so keep in sunniest possible place.

Scorch marks on leaves. Sunscorch. Do not allow leaves to touch glass. Keep in airy place during hot weather as scorching more likely to occur if in stuffy, badly ventilated place.

what goes wrong

White woolly patches appear among leaves. Mealy bug. Remove with small paintbrush dipped in methylated spirits, and spray with insecticide. Repeat 2 or 3 times in growing season.

Leaves shrivel and fall, stem still firm. Too hot and dry in summer or too cold and dry in winter. If too dry in summer, soak in bowl, and in future give more water each time, but allow to dry out between waterings. Keep in more airy place. In winter, keep at 55°F (13°C) and water once a month.

Ceropegia woodii

This is a tuberous rooted plant with hanging stems and heart-shaped leaves, with marks like marbling. The tiny pink and black flowers are like miniature lanterns. It makes a good plant for indoors in a hanging pot. The stems will grow to around 2ft (50–60cm) although they can grow to 8 or 9ft (2½–3m). Most other species make twining stems which need support, although a few are rigid and stick like. All bear flowers of similar structure, but differing in innumerable ways. Other species include *C. stapeliiformis*, with mottled, brown, lizard-like stems, *C. ampliata* with green and white 3in (8cm) long flowers, *C. sandersoniae*, with mottled green and white parachute-like flowers, *C. radicans* with tri-coloured flowers and many others of all shapes, colours and sizes.

Ceropegia woodii, the Rosary vine has round greyish green leaves on stems that trail prettily from a hanging basket. Other Ceropegias can be trained round a hoop or trellis and all produce similar tube-shaped flowers.

Light: The thick tuberous root of this plant prefers to be in shade, while the stems, leaves and flowers prefer to be in full light.
Temperature: Keep a minimum of 40°F (4°C) for safety. Give fresh air in summer.
Water: Water in spring and summer, once a week in hottest months, fortnightly at other times, tail off in autumn, and leave dry in winter. See also Introduction.
Feeding: Use high potash fertilizer once a month in spring and summer.
Soil: Use good loam-based No. 2 potting compost, or soil-less compost, with 30% coarse, gritty sand.
Repotting: Every spring in size larger pot, until 6in (15cm) pot is reached, when soil can be shaken off and plant repotted in same size pot unless tuber has grown too large.
Propagation: By layering stem so that new tuber forms where stem touches soil.

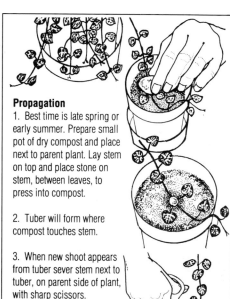

Propagation
1. Best time is late spring or early summer. Prepare small pot of dry compost and place next to parent plant. Lay stem on top and place stone on stem, between leaves, to press into compost.

2. Tuber will form where compost touches stem.

3. When new shoot appears from tuber sever stem next to tuber, on parent side of plant, with sharp scissors.

Leaves fall off, tubers are soft and spongy. Too wet or too cold. Check conditions. Check drainage and compost and water only when plant dries out. Keep dry in winter, above 40°F (4°C).

White woolly patches among leaves. Mealy bug. Remove with small paintbrush dipped in methylated spirits, and spray with contact or systemic insecticide. Repeat 2 or 3 times in growing season.

Leaves limp, then dry up and fall. Too dry. Soak pot in bowl of water for ½ an hour, drain, then water more regularly in hot weather.

Leaves turn black and fall. Stem turns black, roots rot. Too humid. Move to more airy place. Keep dry in winter. Treat roots and stem. (See Introduction.)

Plant shows little sign of growth. Tuber in too light a place or root mealy bug. Check conditions. If white woolly patches on roots, wash all soil off roots, swirl in contact insecticide, and allow to dry for 2–3 days before repotting in fresh compost and clean pot. Leave dry for 2 weeks.

what goes wrong

Leaves turn brown and crisp then fall off. Too hot and stuffy. Give fresh air in summer.

Leaves lose colour, long spaces between pairs. No flowers. Too dark. Gradually move into stronger sunlight over 2 weeks.

Conophytum
spectabile

Conophytums are divided into two main groups: those with large heads of long leaves and those with smaller heads of round leaves. *Conophytum spectabile* is one of the smaller headed types. It has a network of dark markings on the surface and spicily scented flowers. Careful watering is needed and a long dry spell in winter and spring, after which the new heads will emerge as from a chrysalis.

Conophytum spectabile grows to only about 1in (2cm) high and spreads to around 3in (7–8cm). The thick, fleshy leaves shrivel away gradually as a new pair grows between them and must not be removed until they are dry and papery and fall away naturally. The delicate flowers appear between the leaves in late summer or autumn.

Light: Take care in spring when Conophytums are liable to be scorched, especially if a month of cloudy weather is followed by bright sunshine. Shade in spring, reduce shade gradually in early summer to none in autumn.

Temperature: Minimum of 40°F (4°C) in winter; give fresh air in summer.

Water: Conophytums have unusual water requirements. Keep them dry from midwinter to early summer for long-leaved types, to mid-summer for small-leaved. Then water weekly, tailing off to fortnightly in autumn and early winter. During the dry period they will shrivel and look sick but the new body is forming and water at this time is fatal.

Feeding: Not necessary, but if not repotted for 2 or 3 years feed 2 or 3 times in summer with high potash fertilizer.

Soil: Use good loam-based No. 2 potting compost, or soil-less compost, with 50% coarse, gritty sand.

Repotting: Conophytums do not grow well if the roots are disturbed so only repot if not growing or if outgrowing pot.

Propagation: Cut off individual heads with a sharp knife in early summer when plump after first watering. Dust base with hormone rooting powder, dry off for 2 days and place in dry compost. Water after 3 weeks when roots have formed.

Double heads form one inside the other, both still fleshy. Watering started too soon. Leave dry from mid-winter until old head has shrivelled and dried up completely.

Plant light brown and shrivelling on one side. Sun scorch. Shade from strong sunshine. When plant is growing in summer, cut out shrivelled head and dust with fungicide.

what goes wrong

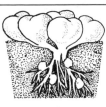

Root mealy bug

1. When repotting, or if plant does not grow but is otherwise healthy, check roots for white woolly patches – root mealy bug.

2. Wash soil off roots if found and swirl in bowl of insecticide diluted with water, following maker's instructions.

3. Leave to dry 2–3 days before repotting in new compost and clean pot.

Plant does not grow. Needs repotting or roots damaged by pests or overwatering. Remove from pot and check roots. If rotting, treat and dry out (see Introduction). If root mealy bug, see right. If clear, repot in fresh compost/grit in clean pot.

All plant heads become brown and papery, but feel firm. Natural in spring and early summer. New head will grow in its place.

Heads elongate in summer, no flowers appear by late summer. Too dark or watered at wrong time. Move gradually to sunnier spot. Keep dry from midwinter to early or midsummer, watering only when old heads have shrivelled to paper thin shells.

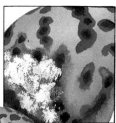

White woolly patches, especially in crevices. Mealy bug. Remove with small paintbrush dipped in methylated spirits, and spray with insecticide. Repeat 2 or 3 times in growing season.

Heads turn black, go soft and rot. Too cold and wet. Keep dry, above 40°F (4°C) in winter. To save plant, pare away blackened part of stem and roots and dust with hormone rooting powder containing fungicide, leave to dry before rerooting in dry compost. Water when new roots appear.

29

Cotyledon undulatum

This attractive meal-covered species with wavy-edged leaves makes a good plant either indoors or in the greenhouse. It can reach 16–20in (40–50cm) tall and 6–8in (15–20cm) across. After four or five years, if grown well, it will produce hanging, bell-shaped pink flowers. Other species include *Cotyledon orbiculata*, with mealy, smooth but red-edged leaves and *C. ladismithiensis*, with fat, green, hairy, wavy-edged leaves. All are fairly simple to grow, but the leaves are sometimes easily dislodged and the mealy covering is easily marked. When using insecticides it is therefore better to choose a systemic type that can be watered into the soil.

Cotyledon undulatum, or Silver crown, is unlikely to flower until it is 4 or 5 years old. Flowers can then appear in spring, summer or autumn but its wavy-edged leaves make the plant attractive all year round.

Light: A sunny spot is best, with no shade, to keep plants compact and well coloured.
Temperature: A minimum of 40°F (4°C), but fewer leaves will fall if kept at 50°F (10°C). Give fresh air in summer.
Water: Start to water once a fortnight in spring, weekly in hottest summer months, tailing off in autumn. If under 50°F (10°C) in winter keep dry, if higher, give a little water monthly. See also Introduction.
Feeding: Use high potash fertilizer once a month in summer only.
Soil: Use good loam-based No. 2 potting compost, or soil-less compost, with 30% coarse, gritty sand.
Repotting: Every spring in size larger pot being careful not to handle leaves, and so mark the floury covering.
Propagation: The leaves will not root. Remove a shoot about 2–3in (8cm) long with a sharp knife, and dust the cut ends with hormone rooting powder. Leave to dry for 2–3 days before inserting in dry compost. Water after 3 weeks when roots have formed. Best time is early summer. Seed is sometimes available.

Brown patches on leaves. Sunscorch — moved into strong light too quickly. Move to shaded place, then back to sunlight over 2 weeks.

White woolly patches among leaves. Mealy bug. Difficult to detect on mealy covering so inspect regularly. Dab in methylated spirits and water systemic insecticide into soil. Do not spray.

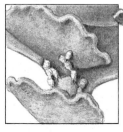

Repotting

When repotting, take care not to damage the soft floury covering. Prepare new pot one size larger than old. Ease plant out sideways onto surface padded with newspaper, grasping root-ball not plant body. Lower gently into new pot and firm compost around roots. Do not water again for 2–3 weeks.

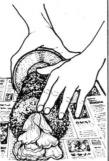

Leaves drop off leaving topknot on each stem. Many causes. May be too dry, need feeding or repotting or overwatering may have caused black rot. If dry in summer, soak pot for ½ hour in bowl of water, then drain and water more generously each time. In winter water monthly. If roots rotted, pare away soft area (see Introduction) and repot. If all conditions correct, check for root mealy bug .

Leaves, stems and roots black and rotting, leaves fall. Too cold and wet, too humid. Move to warmer place, over 50°F (10°C) in winter and allow soil to dry out. Give just enough water to stop leaves shrivelling — once a month enough. Pare away blackened stem and roots and dust with fungicide before rerooting (see Introduction).

what goes wrong

If stems grow tall they may become topheavy, and may lean and flop over. Insert cane beside plant to support it or repropagate from shoots.

Long gaps between leaves, leaves pale with thin mealy covering. Too dark. Move to lighter place over 2 weeks.

Marks on leaves, meal rubbed off. Damage by humans, curtains or pets. Move to protected place and plant will recover.

Round pieces missing from edges of leaves, lower stem thickened and no new growth. Vine weevil. Dust soil with insecticide powder. Slice stem from base until brown area in centre removed. Dust with fungicide and leave to dry. Inspect roots for damage and treat as stem. Reroot in dry compost.

31

Crassula ovata

This plant is among the larger and more showy species of Crassula: it can easily grow to 3ft (1m) tall. It is often labelled wrongly *Crassula portulacea* and is commonly known as the jade tree. It has shiny jade green, spoon-shaped leaves, sometimes with red edges. On mature plants that get plenty of sunlight in winter, clusters of star-shaped pink or white flowers 2–3in (6–8cm) across are produced. Another large one is *Crassula arborescens* with disc-like silvery-green leaves. *C. falcata* and *C. lactea* will make plants a foot (30cm) tall or wide. Smaller Crassulas include *C.* 'Morgan's Beauty', *C. columella*, *C. nealeana*, *C. cornuta*, *C. arta*, *C. deceptor*, *C. socialis*, *C. justi-corderoyi*, *C. cooperi*, *C. pubescens*, *C. teres*, *C. tecta* and many more.

The smaller Crassulas, including this *Crassula* 'Morgan's Beauty', flower more quickly than the large *Crassula ovata* (right). They are also useful where space is limited as many will never outgrow a 4 or 5in (10 or 12cm) pot. The striking flowers appear in winter and last a week or more.

Light: A light, sunny position is needed.
Temperature: A minimum of 40°F (4°C). Give fresh air in summer.
Water: Start watering fortnightly in spring, weekly in hottest months, tailing off in autumn. Give just a little every month to prevent leaves shrivelling in winter. See also Introduction.
Feeding: Not necessary, unless plant has not been repotted in spring. If not, use high potash fertilizer 2 or 3 times in summer.
Soil: Use good loam-based No. 2 potting compost, or soil-less compost, with 30% coarse, gritty sand.
Repotting: Every spring in size larger pot.
Propagation: In spring or summer shoots of 3–4 leaves can be removed with a sharp knife, dried for a day or two and inserted in or laid on dry compost. Water after 2–3 weeks when roots have appeared. Individual leaves may be gently prised off and treated similarly and will form new plants.

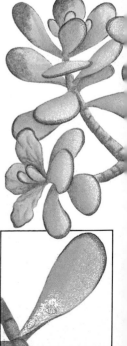

Brown marks on leaves. Sunscorch, moved into bright sun too quickly. Move out of sun, then reintroduce over period of 2 weeks. Give fresh air in summer.

Leaves distorted, as virus. Reaction to insecticide, especially malathion. Stop using insecticide and plant will recover.

White woolly patches among leaves. Mealy bug. Remove with small paintbrush dipped in methylated spirits and spray with contact or systemic insecticide. Repeat 2–3 times in growing season.

Leaves turn black and fall, stem and roots rot. Black rot — too cold and wet. Keep above 40°F (4°C) in winter, best around 50°F (10°C). Allow to dry out. Pare away blackened area and dust with fungicide. Leave to dry for 2–3 days before rerooting in dry compost.

Stems grow long with long spaces between leaves, and bend towards light. Too dark. Keep in full sunlight all year round. ·

Leaves dry up and drop. Some leaf-fall natural in winter. In summer, too dry or overwatered. If dry, give more water at each watering. If wet, allow to dry out thoroughly.

what goes wrong

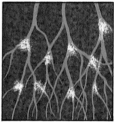

Plant does not grow. Needs feeding or repotting. If conditions correct, check roots for root mealy bug (white woolly patches). Wash all soil off roots and swirl in contact insecticide. Allow to dry before repotting in fresh compost and clean pot. Leave dry for 2 weeks.

Round pieces missing from edges of leaves, little new growth, stem swollen. Vine weevil. Dust soil with insecticide powder. Slice stem from base until brown central area with larvae reached. Dust with fungicide and reroot (see Introduction).

33

Dudleya brittonii

This species is one of the several which are covered with a mealy coating as a protection against the drying effect of the sun. This covering is easily marked by handling the leaves, or by careless watering. The plant needs to be watered either by filling a saucer in which the pot stands, or by pouring the water carefully around the edge of the plant so that it does not fall on the leaves. Sunshine is needed to bring out the best colouring. They nearly all come from Mexico where they grow on hillsides and show up as white patches on the grey-brown rock. They will reach a height of 3–4in (8–10cm) and about 8–10in (20–25cm) across. Other species include *D. albiflora, D. candida, D. densiflora*: none of these is readily available, but can be obtained from time to time.

Dudleya brittonii's intense white colouring comes from a powdery coating which protects it from drying out in bright sunlight. To avoid damaging it, always water from the base of the pot and do not spray with insecticides. Flowers are rare indoors.

Light: A sunny position is needed to keep plants in good shape and encourage dense white mealy covering.

Temperature: A minimum of 45°F (7°C) is needed for safety. Give fresh air in summer.

Water: In spring and early summer water fortnightly, weekly in hottest months. Tail off to little water in autumn and in winter water once a month to stop drying out. See also Introduction.

Feeding: Use high potash fertilizer 2 or 3 times in summer.

Soil: Use good loam-based No. 2 potting compost, or soil-less compost, with 40% coarse, gritty sand.

Repotting: Every spring in size larger half-pot or pan, being careful not to handle leaves at all, as the mealy covering is easily marked and the appearance spoiled.

Propagation: Leaves will not root and form fresh plants but whole rosettes can be separated with a sharp knife.

Leaves are marked, mealy covering removed in patches or on edges. Damaged by humans, curtains, or perhaps cats, brushing against plants. Will recover if moved to safe position.

Plant does not grow. Needs feeding or, if white woolly patches on roots, root mealy bug. Wash soil off roots, swirl in contact insecticide, and allow to dry before repotting in fresh compost and washed pot. Leave dry for 2 weeks. Feed 2–3 times in summer.

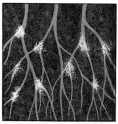

Mealy covering not very thick or white, no flowers. Not enough sunlight. Move to lighter position in sunny window.

Leaves blacken and fall, stem rots. Too cold and wet, too humid. Move to warmer, more airy position and allow to dry out before watering again. Keep dry in winter.

what goes wrong

Woolly patches on leaves. Mealy bug, difficult to see on this plant so inspect regularly. Dab with a small paintbrush just dipped in methylated spirits, and water systemic insecticide into soil. Do not spray.

Leaves long and pale in winter. Too hot, damp and humid. Move to more airy place and allow to dry out thoroughly. Keep dry in winter, even in normal room temperatures.

Propagation

1. After a few years, some Dudleyas will form clumps of rosettes. Individual rosettes can be separated from rest with sharp knife. Take care not to damage plant's floury covering when handling it.

2. Dust cut surfaces with hormone rooting powder to prevent infection and leave cutting to dry for 2 days before potting in small individual pot. Do not water for 2–3 weeks.

Brown scorch marks on leaves. Plant has been moved into direct sunlight too quickly. Move out of direct sun, then bring back gradually over 2 weeks. Make sure ventilation is good.

Leaves have chewed edges, lower stem swollen; plant does not grow well. Vine weevil. Dust around base of pot with insecticide powder and water soil with systemic insecticide to kill larvae in stem. Or, slice from base of stem until larvae discovered and reroot (see Introduction).

Leaves marked with small spots of green. Insecticide spray has damaged mealy covering. Water systemic insecticides into soil. Do not spray.

Lower leaves dry up. Too dry. Soak pot in bowl of water for ½ an hour, then drain. Water regularly in hot weather, whenever soil dries out.

Duvalia corderoyi

This low growing plant spreads and each year produces several new shoots from which its extraordinary flowers appear in summer and autumn. They vary from species to species, some flowers being barely ½ in (1cm) across, while some more tropical ones are about 1½in (3cm) wide. *D. corderoyi* is one of the medium-sized species and like the others has a flower with an intricate, hairy centre which is attractive to flies. The plant itself will grow to about 1½in (3–4cm) high and spread to around 6 or 8in (15–20cm). Other species include *Duvalia sulcata*, with larger pink or brownish-pink flowers, needing high temperatures; *D. angustiloba*, with the tiniest dark brown flowers; *D. pillansii*, with deep red flowers and *D. elegans*, with almost black flowers. None of them is difficult to cultivate.

Duvalia corderoyi. The star-fish shaped flowers are this Duvalia's main attraction and to make sure that they appear, always keep the plant in a very sunny position. When taking cuttings, do not remove too many of the young, freshly developed shoots as it is on these that flowers are produced.

Light: A sunny position is needed to keep leaves compact and encourage flowering.

Temperature: A minimum of 40°F (4°C), but best to keep above 50°F (10°C) as one or two species need warmer conditions.

Water: Water fortnightly in spring and summer, weekly in hottest months, allowing to dry out between waterings; tail off in autumn and keep dry in winter. See also Introduction.

Feeding: Unnecessary if repotted in spring. If not, use high potash fertilizer 2 or 3 times in summer.

Soil: Use good loam-based No. 2 potting compost, or soil-less compost, with 40% coarse, gritty sand.

Repotting: Every spring in fresh soil in size larger pot. After 4–5 years use only young shoots and discard older stems.

Propagation: By cutting at natural junction of young stems with old. Also possible from seed but not easily obtained.

what goes wrong

Plant collapsing or not growing, black flies around plant and soil. Sciara fly. Inspect roots and if rotted, pare back until all trace of rot or larvae removed. Then treat and repot (see Introduction).

Stems turn yellow, then black in winter. Too cold. Is plant shut behind curtains at night? Move to warmer place, above 40°F (4°C).

Taking cuttings

1. Take cuttings after flowering. Cut off a new stem where it joins old with a sharp knife.

2. Dust base of new stem and cut end of old with hormone rooting powder to prevent infection and leave cutting to dry for 2 days.

3. Prepare new pot and place cutting on top of dry compost. Do not water for 2–3 weeks, when roots begin to show at base.

Stems black and shrivelled, some fall over. Too cold, wet and humid. Allow to dry out thoroughly and keep above 40°F (4°C) in winter. Pare away rot from stem. If roots black and rotted, treat and repot (see Introduction). Or, take cuttings from healthy stems.

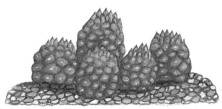

Stems grow tall and pale, especially at tips. Few flowers. Too dark. Move into full light over 2 weeks.

Brown scorch marks on stems. Sunscorch, plant moved in to direct sun too quickly in stuffy place. Move out of direct light, then return gradually over 2 weeks. Keep in more airy place.

Stems shrivel and dry. Many possible reasons. Too hot and dry in winter; too dry in summer, needs feeding or root mealy bug. If soil dry, increase amount of water each time but allow to dry out between. In winter moisten soil monthly and keep around 50°F (10°C). If feeding and soil correct, check roots for white woolly patches. Swirl roots in insecticide, allow to dry before repotting in fresh compost and clean pot. Leave dry for 2 weeks.

Stems shrivel, white woolly patches especially round base near soil. Mealy bug. Remove with small paintbrush dipped in methylated spirits, and spray with contact or systemic insecticide. Repeat 2 or 3 times in growing season.

37

Echeveria agavoides

This plant is grown for the beauty of its waxy-leaved rosette, which is grey-green with red edges to the leaves. It grows to a height of about 4in (10cm) and the rosettes reach about 6in (15cm) across. Echeverias come from Central America and vary from tiny inch-wide (2–3cm) rosettes to large shrubby plants standing 3ft (1m) tall with rosettes 2ft (60cm) across. The leaves vary from pale green, through all sorts of blues, greys and purple shades with a bloom on them that is easily damaged. Other species include *Echeveria affinis* with almost black leaves; *E. minima*, small blue, red-edged rosettes; *E. setosa* with hairy, green leaves; *E. pulvinata*, velvety green, red-edged leaves.

Echeveria agavoides. These attractive flowers grow on a 6in (15cm) stem which grows from among the rosette of leaves. A collection of different Echeveria species makes a colourful display as the leaves may be powder blue, green, grey, lilac or almost pink. This species will redden, especially along the leaf edges in a sunny position.

Light: A sunny position is needed to bring out the best colouring.

Temperature: Keep at 45°F (7°C). Give fresh air in summer.

Water: Water fortnightly in spring and summer, weekly in hottest weather, so that soil does not dry out completely. In autumn and winter give just enough once a month to stop leaves shrivelling. See also Introduction.

Feeding: Use high potash fertilizer in summer once a month.

Soil: Use a good loam-based No. 2 potting or soil-less compost, with 20% coarse, gritty sand.

Repotting: Every spring in size larger pot or larger if plant has grown well, using half pots or pans for the shallow roots, and being careful not to handle leaves and spoil the mealy or waxy covering.

Propagation: Most will make fresh plants from healthy leaves. Remove and dry for a day or two, then lay on top of dry compost. Give water after 2 weeks when leaves have roots, and plantlet formed at base.

White woolly patches between the leaves and on the stem, where young shoots are appearing. Mealy bug. Remove with small paintbrush dipped in methylated spirits, and spray with pyrethrum-based insecticide.

Round pieces missing from leaf edges, stem swollen, little new growth. Vine weevil. Sprinkle insecticide powder around base of pot and water soil with systemic insecticide to kill larvae in stem. Or slice stem from base until larvae found and reroot. (See Introduction.)

Leaves marked in patches or at edge. Coating damaged by handling. Unsightly but not fatal.

Small insects on flowers or buds. Greenfly. Spray with pyrethrum-based insecticide and repeat in 10 days if not clear.

what goes wrong

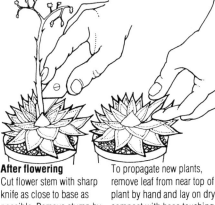

After flowering
Cut flower stem with sharp knife as close to base as possible. Remove stump by gently pulling out when absolutely dry.

To propagate new plants, remove leaf from near top of plant by hand and lay on dry compost with base touching surface. Roots will appear and new plantlet will grow at base.

Leaves and stem turn black. Leaves pull out easily. Too cold and wet. Keep no lower than 45°F (7°C) in winter in dry compost. Treat stem (see Introduction). If plant does not recover, use healthy leaves for cuttings.

Leaves distorted. Caused by excessive use of insecticides. Use only pyrethrum-based insecticides. Not fatal.

Leaves small and few. Needs repotting, or if soil dry, more water. Soak pot in bowl of water, drain, then give more water each time. but always allow to dry out between waterings.

Plant elongates in centre, leaves pale green. Too little light, move gradually over 2 weeks to a sunny spot. If too hot and wet in winter, leaves may grow like this then rot. Try to keep below 50°F (10°C) in winter with just enough water monthly to prevent leaves from shrivelling.

Plant does not grow, and on repotting white woolly patches found on roots. Root mealy bug. Wash all soil off roots, swirl in contact insecticide and allow to dry before repotting in fresh compost and clean pot. Leave dry for 2 weeks.

Leaves shrivel in winter. Too dry. Moisten soil once a month to prevent drying out completely but always make sure pot dries right out in between. Try to keep cool (under 50°F, 10°C) in winter.

39

Euphorbia milii

This popular plant grows into a small thorny shrub, which branches freely and flowers readily with red or yellow flowers. It will reach a height of 12–16in (30–40cm) with a width of 8–12in (20–30cm). Beware of the sap in all Euphorbias, which is an extreme irritant and dangerous to the eyes. This is a vast genus with well over a thousand succulent species, most of which are too large for indoor culture. Good small species include *E. obesa, E. suzannae E. decaryi, E. aeruginosa* and many others.

Light: A sunny position on a windowsill or in a greenhouse is needed for best results.
Temperature: A minimum of 45°F (7°C) is needed, but for safety some species prefer 50°F (10°C). Give fresh air in summer.
Water: Start watering in spring, fortnightly through spring and summer, weekly in hottest months, but allow to dry out between waterings. Tail off in autumn, and keep dry in winter, when leaves will fall. See also Introduction.
Feeding: Use high potash fertilizer in summer 2 or 3 times.
Soil: Use good loam-based No. 2 potting compost, or soil-less compost, with 30% coarse, gritty sand.
Repotting: Every spring in size larger pot, until 5 or 6in (15cm) pot is reached, when soil may be shaken off roots and plant repotted in same size pot with fresh soil. Do not water for 2 weeks after repotting.
Propagation: Cut off pieces of stem 2–3in (5–7cm) long in spring or summer, with a sharp knife. Dip cutting in water for a moment to stem flow of milky sap. Dust lightly with hormone rooting powder, leave to dry and after 3 days place in dry compost. Water after 3 weeks, when roots have started. Wash hands well after contact with sap.

Euphorbia milii, commonly known as the Crown of thorns, can vary in size from 1ft (30cm) tall to some with a spread of 6ft (2m). Its spiky stems have bright green, fleshy leaves which fall in winter if the temperature is below 55°F (13°C). The red 'flowers' are in fact coloured leaves called bracts. The true flower is the small yellow centre.

what goes wrong

Leaves dry up and fall. In winter, if below 55°F (13°C), natural. New leaves will grow in spring. If temperature higher, water once a month to retain leaves. In summer, overwatered or badly drained. Allow soil to dry out between waterings or roots may rot. If paring away damaged roots, take care as sap will run. Dip roots in water to stem sap flow.

40

Stem very thin at growing point; leaves pale greenish-yellow. Too dark or in winter too hot or too wet. Move gradually to sunny spot over 2 weeks. In winter keep dry and airy.

White marks on leaves. Caused by either insecticide spray or hard water leaving lime marks. It will not harm the plant.

Taking cuttings
When taking stem cuttings wear gloves to protect hands from poisonous sap. Cut 2–3in (5–8cm) tip in spring or early summer, just below a leaf. Remove lowest leaves if close to cut end and dip stem end in water to stop sap flowing. Drip water onto cut end on plant as well to seal.

Leaves scorched and shrivelled in summer. Too hot and dry. Move to more airy place and water when soil dries out in hot weather.

Leaves very lush but few flowers. Overfeeding. Stop feeding until next spring. Feed only 2 or 3 times in spring and summer.

Black sooty dust below where flowers have been. Sooty mould forming on the nectar. Spray weekly while flowering to dilute nectar and include a systemic fungicide in spray once a month. Dust off mould when dry.

Leaves blacken and fall, stem ends turn black and go soft, roots rot. Too humid. Move to more airy place and pare away damaged stem and roots. Dust with hormone rooting powder and leave to dry 2–3 days before rerooting. (see Introduction.)

Plants show little sign of growth, white woolly patches on roots. Root mealy bug. Wash all soil off roots, swirl in contact insecticide, and allow to dry before repotting in fresh compost and clean pot. Leave dry for 2 weeks.

41

Faucaria tigrina

There are several species of this South African genus available, all commonly called Tiger's jaws. They make good plants for a bright windowsill display or for a greenhouse. Bright, dandelion-yellow flowers are produced in late or early autumn. They grow in clumps to fill a 5 or 6in (15cm) half-pot or pan in about 4 or 5 years and reach about 2in (5cm) tall. There is one white-flowered species not at all easy to obtain, called *Faucaria candicans*. But other good yellow-flowered species include *F. albidens* with attractive, white-edged leaves and teeth, *F. tuberculosa*, very popular for its 'fierce' teeth and swollen leaves, *F. kingiae* and *F. britteniae* somewhat similar to *F. tigrina*. All are easy to grow, provided you are careful to water at the right time of year.

Faucaria albidens. Faucarias are known as Tiger's jaws as their pairs of fleshy, spiked leaves are said to look like a tiger's open mouth. The bright yellow flowers appear in late summer and autumn but like most succulents, they will not produce them if they have been kept too hot or too wet in the previous winter months.

Light: A sunny position is needed to keep good colour and to ensure flowering.

Temperature: A minimum of 40°F (4°C) is needed. Give fresh air in summer.

Water: Start watering in spring, about once a fortnight, weekly in hottest months. Tail off in autumn, keep dry in winter. See also Introduction.

Feeding: Not necessary if repotted in spring, but if not, use high potash fertilizer 2 or 3 times in summer.

Soil: Use good loam-based No. 2 potting compost, or soil-less compost, with 30% coarse, gritty sand.

Repotting: Every year in spring, in size larger half-pot or pan. Try not to disturb roots too much. Do not water for 2 weeks.

Propagation: Take cuttings of whole shoots in spring and summer with a sharp knife. Dust them with hormone rooting powder, leave 3 days to dry before placing the base on or just in dry compost. Water after 3 weeks when roots have formed.

Flowers shrivel quickly and have brown edges. Too dry in summer or in too much strong sun. Check soil and water when soil dries out in hot weather. Protect from strong midday summer sun.

Rusty spots on leaves. Tiny webs. Red spider mite. Spray with insecticide and repeat every 2 weeks for 3 months. To prevent attack, spray regularly 2–3 times a year.

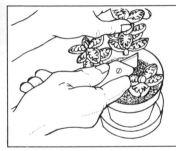

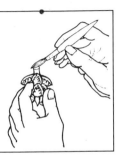

Taking cuttings

1. Cut off whole shoots with sharp knife in spring, cutting straight across stem.

2. Dust cut surfaces with hormone rooting powder to prevent infection and leave cutting to dry for 2–3 days. Place on dry compost and do not water until roots appear.

what goes wrong

Stems long with pale leaves, no flowers by late summer. Too dark or too hot in winter. Move over 2 weeks into full sunlight and keep in airy place. Keep below 50°F (10°C) in winter.

No sign of growth, though conditions correct. Check roots for root mealy bug — white woolly patches on roots. Wash all soil off roots, swirl roots in contact insecticide, and allow to dry before repotting in fresh compost and washed pot. Leave dry for 2 weeks.

Leaves shrivel, plant loses colour and does not grow in summer. Too dry or needs feeding or repotting. Check soil. If dry, soak in bowl of water for ½ hour, then drain. Repot in spring and feed 2–3 times in summer. In winter leaves shrivel naturally.

White woolly patches among leaves. Mealy bug. Remove with small paintbrush dipped in methylated spirits, and spray with contact or systemic insecticide. Repeat 2 or 3 times in growing season.

Leaves turn black and shrivel. Black rot, roots rotting. Too cold and wet or too humid. Keep over 40°F (4°C) in winter. Pare off blackened stem and dust with fungicide. Keep dry.

Brown scorch marks. Sun scorch. Move out of direct sun, then return gradually to sunny, more airy spot over 2 weeks. If in winter, may be natural shrivelling of leaves.

43

Fenestraria rhopalophylla

There are two forms of this species, one with yellow flowers the other with white. There is also a very similar purple-pink flowered plant called *Frithia pulchra*. All have extraordinary sausage-shaped leaves with transparent ends which let in light and form tight packed bunches growing close to the soil. In the wild in South Africa, only the transparent tips of the leaves show and even then only at soil level; the rest of the plant is below ground. The yellow flowered form is sometimes labelled *Fenestraria aurantiaca*, or *F. rhopalophylla v. aurantiaca*.

Fenestraria rhopalophylla, known as Baby's toes, is wonderfully suited to survival in very dry areas. In times of drought its leaves pull themselves right down into the soil so that just the transparent leaf ends show. Light is still able to penetrate to the plant through these 'windows'.

Light: A sunny position is necessary for compact growth and to induce flowering.

Temperature: A minimum of 40°F (4°C) is needed. Give fresh air in summer.

Water: Water fortnightly in spring and summer but not overhead, weekly in hottest weather. Allow to dry between waterings. Tail off in autumn, keep dry in winter.

Feeding: If not repotted in spring, use high potash fertilizer 2 or 3 times in summer. Unnecessary if repotted that year.

Soil: Use good loam-based No. 2 potting compost, or soil-less compost, with 30% coarse, gritty sand.

Repotting: Every year in spring in size larger pot, being careful not to disturb roots too much. Leave dry for 2 weeks after repotting.

Propagation: Plant can be divided into small clumps, but individual leaves will not root to form new plants. Cut clump apart with sharp knife, dust cut surfaces with hormone rooting powder and leave dry for 3 days before repotting in fresh dry compost. Water after 3 weeks. Also fairly easily raised from seed.

Stems grow long and floppy, separating from each other and turning pale green. In winter, too hot and wet. Move to cooler position, around 50°F (10°C) in winter and allow to dry out completely, giving no water from late autumn to spring. In summer, too dark. Keep in full light to improve colour and shape.

what goes wrong

Stems shrink back into soil so only tips are exposed. Rare indoors, caused by too much light. Shade in hottest midsummer days.

Stems do not grow in spring and summer. Needs feeding or repotting. Repot in fresh compost and feed 2–3 times in growing season.

No growth though conditions correct. Stems shrink. Check roots for root mealy bug. If found, wash soil off roots and swirl in insecticide. Dry before repotting in fresh compost and clean pot. Leave dry for 2 weeks.

Individual stems dry up. Too dry or water on stems. Water from below and give more at each watering in spring and summer. Check compost regularly in hot weather.

Stems light brown and shrivelled on side nearest window. Sunscorch. Shade, then move back gradually over 2 weeks into bright sun. New stems may grow in place of damaged one. Brown marks may also be caused by cold. Keep above 40°F (4°C) in winter, away from glass.

Stems lose colour. Too dark. Move into full sunlight over 2 week period. Keep in full light all year round, only shading on hottest summer days if stems begin to shrink back into soil.

Growing from seed

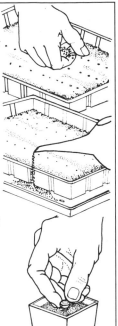

1. Sow seed thinly in spring on surface of prepared tray or half-pot. Tap sides to settle seed.

2. Water from base with fungicide diluted as for 'damping off' of seedlings, until surface is damp. Place tray or pot in polythene bag with ends folded underneath to seal in moisture. Leave in light (not direct sun) at 70°F (21°C). Do not water again unless condensation on polythene becomes patchy or dries.

3. Prick out after 6 months into 2in (5cm) pots or ½in (2cm) apart in trays.

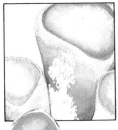

White woolly patches on stems. Mealy bug. Remove with small paintbrush dipped in methylated spirits and spray with insecticide. Repeat 2–3 times in growing season.

All stems shrivel. In summer much too dry. In winter, natural in dry resting period. In summer soak pot in bowl of water for ½ hour, drain then give more water each time.

Stems black and soft. Too cold, wet or humid. Move to warmer place, around 50°F (10°C) in winter and allow to dry out thoroughly. In summer always allow to dry out between waterings. Pare off blackened stem and dust with fungicide.

Gasteria liliputana

This small, rosette-forming species belongs to a genus of larger plants, some of which grow to 2 or 3ft (1m) tall. *Gasteria liliputana* is easy to grow and puts up with a lot of neglect; but if treated well it will make a clump of stems in 3 or 4 years, and produce dainty pink and green flowers. Others worth growing include *Gasteria batesiana*, with gnarled, reptile-like leaves, *G. armstrongii*, with its blackish-green leaves and slow-growth and the heavily spotted *G. verrucosa*.

Light: A sunny position is necessary for good growth and flowering if indoors, but in a greenhouse, some shading will be necessary if over 90°F (32°C).

Temperature: A minimum of 40°F (4°C) is needed. Give fresh air in summer.

Water: Fortnightly in spring and summer, weekly in hottest months. Continue until late autumn, reducing amount and frequency until completely dry by early winter. See also Introduction.

Feeding: Use high potash fertilizer 3 or 4 times in summer months.

Soil: Use good loam-based No. 2 potting compost, or soil-less compost, with 30% coarse, gritty sand.

Repotting: Every spring in size larger pot or larger still if good growth has been made. Keep dry for 2 weeks after repotting.

Propagation: In spring cut off whole shoots (with roots) with sharp knife and replant or cut off single leaves. Do not use those around base. Dust cut end of leaf with hormone rooting powder, leave to dry for 3 days then place on dry compost. Water after 3 weeks when roots have formed. After about 8 weeks, new shoots will appear from base. Do not remove old leaf until quite dried up.

Gasteria liliputana's pink and green flowers appear in spring and early summer. Its scientific name Gasteria (from the latin word for stomach), comes from the flowers' stomach-like shape. This small species grows only a couple of inches high, though others in the genus may be up to 3ft (1m) tall.

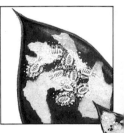

White woolly patches among leaves. Mealy bug. Remove with small paintbrush dipped in methylated spirits and spray with insecticide. Repeat 2 or 3 times in growing season.

Leaves marked purplish-brown. Too much sunlight. Move to slightly more shaded position.

Leaves blacken and fall, roots rot. Black rot. Too cold and wet. Move to warmer place and in summer only water when dried out. In winter, keep dry.

Lower leaves turn brown, shrivel and fall. Sun scorch. Too hot and dry. Move to cooler place and in hot weather water whenever soil dries out, about once a week.

Leaves long thin and light greenish-yellow; no flowers. Too dark. Move gradually to sunnier spot over 2 weeks. Or, if kept moist in winter, too hot. Allow to dry out in winter.

Few leaves, little new growth. Needs feeding or repotting. Repot annually in fresh compost and feed monthly in summer.

Propagation
In spring cut off single leaves from centre of plant with sharp knife, cutting as close to base of leaf as possible. Rosettes growing as offsets beside main stem can be removed in the same way.

Round limpet-like patches on leaves. Scale insect. Spray and soak soil with systemic insecticide. After 2 weeks pick insects off with a sharp point e.g. a toothpick.

Flowers shrivel quickly, leaves shrivel. In summer, too dry. Give more water but allow to dry out between waterings. In winter, leaves shrivel naturally if dry, to conserve moisture.

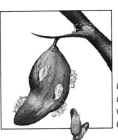

Green insects on flower buds or flowers. Greenfly. Spray with insecticide and repeat every 2 weeks until clear.

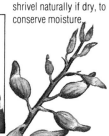

what goes wrong

Black spots on leaves. Cause not clear, physiological disorder. Cut out affected leaves and try putting in less sunny place and watering more often.

Leaf tips dry up and turn light brown, little growth. Too dry and too stuffy. Give more water with each watering but allow to dry out between. Move to more airy place.

Plant grows slowly, white woolly patches on roots when repotting. Root mealy bug. Wash soil off roots and swirl in contact insecticide. Allow to dry before repotting in fresh compost and washed pot. Leave dry for 2 weeks.

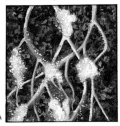

Gibbaeum dispar

This South African plant is awkward to grow since unlike most succulents, it grows in late autumn and winter, generally producing its purple-red flowers in spring. It therefore needs a different watering programme from most other succulents, which have their dry, dormant period in winter. It grows to about 1½in (3cm) tall and covers a base area of 4in (10cm). Other species, not easy to obtain, but worth seeking out from specialist nurseries, are *G. album*, with white or pink flowers, *G. pubescens* or *G. shandii* with violet-red flowers, and *G. velutinum* with lilac-pink flowers. All are winter growers and need the same treatment.

Light: Full sun, especially in autumn and winter when buds are forming.
Temperature: Winter minimum 45°F (7°C). Give fresh air in summer.
Water: Read the general instructions in the introduction, but remember that this plant's resting period is late spring/early summer, not winter. After flowering, leave dry for 4–6 weeks, then start watering fortnightly in late summer. In autumn and winter water monthly, increasing to fortnightly in early spring.
Feeding: Not necessary unless plant has not been repotted for 2 years. Then feed with a high potash liquid fertilizer once when watering in autumn.
Soil: Use good loam-based No. 2 potting compost, or soil-less compost, with 40% coarse, gritty sand.
Repotting: Only every 3 years to change soil, or when roots fill the pot. Use half-pots or pans. Do not water for 3 weeks after repotting.
Propagation: Separate heads with sharp knife in summer to use as cuttings. Growing from seed is difficult.

Gibbaeum dispar. Gibbaeums grow in winter and their special watering needs must be carefully met. They will only flower if kept in a very sunny position, especially in autumn and winter when the flower buds are forming between the pairs of fleshy green leaves.

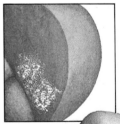

White woolly patches appear among leaves. Mealy bug. Remove with small paintbrush dipped in methylated spirits, and spray with insecticide. Repeat 2 or 3 times in growing season.

Plant turns light brown and shrivels on side nearest glass. Scorched. Move away from glass, so that air can circulate between plant and glass. Watch out in spring for sudden bright sunny spells, and shade plants for a week to accustom them to the sudden sunshine. If heads have completely dried out carefully cut them out.

Treating roots

1. Though a small plant above the surface, Gibbaeum has thick turnip-like roots. Check when repotting for root mealy bug.

2. If found, wash soil off roots and soak in bowl of insecticide diluted as maker recommends. Leave to dry for 2 days.

3. Repot in dry compost and clean pot. Do not water again for 2–3 weeks to allow plant's roots to grow into new compost.

No flowers. Not uncommon, needs a very sunny position. Try putting outside for summer months but protect from rainfall.

Leaves lose colour and grow tall in spring/summer. Watered at wrong time of year. Keep dry for 4–6 weeks from late spring but make sure light is good.

Little growth, leaves shrivel. In summer during rest period, natural. In spring, needs repotting. In autumn, needs feeding once. In winter, too dry. Water just enough to keep leaves plump, especially when buds forming. Once a month enough.

Plant shows little sign of growth, and on repotting white woolly patches are on roots. Root mealy bug. Wash all soil off roots, swirl in contact insecticide, and allow to dry before repotting in fresh compost and clean pot. Leave dry for two weeks.

Brown limpet-like spots. Scale insect. Spray with insecticide, and pick off scales after a week or two. Spray again after a month.

what goes wrong

Irregular brown spots and patches. Too cold in winter. Keep in warmer conditions (over 45°F, 7°C). Not usually fatal.

Plant elongates, gapes, becoming yellowish-green. Too little light, move gradually over 2 weeks to sunnier spot. Needs full sun in autumn and winter when buds are forming. In poor light, plant will fail to flower.

Plant shrivels, then turns black and soft, usually in winter. Too cold or overwatered. Keep above 45°F (7°C) in winter and water monthly, allowing soil to dry out thoroughly. Keep dry in summer. A humid atmosphere will cause rot so do not spray and keep in light, airy place.

49

Graptopetalum bellum

This beautiful flowering succulent (also known as *Tacitus bellus*) was only discovered in the last ten years or so, but is already a widespread and popular plant. It grows to about 2in (4cm) tall and spreads to 4–6in (10–15cm). Others often available are *Graptopetalum pachyphyllum*, with tiny, blue-green, darker tipped leaves, *G. paraguayense*, with greyish-white leaves and *G. filiferum*, green and red leaves with wispy bristles. All are fairly easy to grow.

Light: A sunny position is needed for flowering and to keep the plant in a flat rosette.
Temperature: Minimum 40°F (4°C). Give fresh air in summer.
Water: Water fortnightly in spring and summer, weekly in the hottest months; allow to dry out between waterings. Tail off in autumn, and keep dry in winter. See also Introduction.
Feeding: Use a high potash fertilizer 2 or 3 times in summer months.
Soil: Use good loam-based No. 2 potting compost, or soil-less compost, with 30% coarse, gritty sand.
Repotting: Every spring in size larger half-pot or pan. When 6in (15cm) pot is reached shake off soil carefully and repot in same sized pot with fresh soil. Do not water for 2 weeks after repotting.
Propagation: Whole offshoots can be cut off in spring and summer with a sharp knife, or leaves gently pulled away. Do not use leaves from base. Dust with hormone rooting powder, leave to dry for 3 days, and plant in dry compost. Water after 3 weeks when roots have formed. Small plants will appear around the base of the rooted leaf after 3 or 4 more weeks. Do not remove old leaf until dried up.

Graptopetalum bellum. Most Graptopetalums have creamy-white flowers so the bright pink blooms of this species make it very striking. They appear in late spring and early summer, opening one after the other so that a clump may be in flower for a week or 10 days.

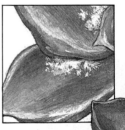

White woolly patches between leaves and where young shoots are appearing. Mealy bug. Remove with small paintbrush dipped in methylated spirits, and spray with pyrethrum-based insecticide.

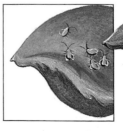

Small insects on flowers, buds or leaves. Greenfly. Spray with pyrethrum-based insecticide and repeat in 10 days if not clear.

Leaves shrivel. Too dry. Moisten soil once a month in winter to prevent drying out. In summer, water when soil is dry.

Plant elongates in centre, leaves pale green, no flowers in spring/summer. Too little light or in winter, too hot and wet. Move gradually over 2 weeks to a sunny spot. Keep around 50°F (10°C) in winter, watering just enough monthly to keep leaves plump.

Leaves small and few. Needs repotting or feeding, or if soil dry, more water. Soak pot in bowl of water drain, then give more water each time, but always allow to dry out between waterings. Repot in spring and feed 2–3 times in summer.

Round pieces missing from leaf edges, base swollen, little new growth. Vine weevil. Sprinkle insecticide powder around base of pot and water soil with systemic insecticide to kill larvae in stem. Or slice stem from base until larvae found and reroot. (See Introduction).

Plant does not grow, and on repotting white woolly patches found on roots. Root mealy bug. Wash all soil off roots, swirl in contact insecticide and allow to dry before repotting in fresh compost and clean pot. Leave dry for 2 weeks.

what goes wrong

Leaves die back, scorch marks. Sunscorch. Move out of sun, then gradually back over 2 weeks. Give fresh air in summer.

When flowers have died, leave until quite dry and shrivelled. Stalk will pull away easily by hand.

Leaves marked in patches or at edge. Cutting damaged by handling. Unsightly but not fatal.

Leaves distorted. Caused by excessive use of insecticides. Use only pyrethrum-based insecticides. Not fatal.

Leaves turn black and pull out easily. Too cold and wet. Keep no lower than 45°F (7°C) in winter in dry compost. If roots rotted, treat and reroot (see Introduction). If plant does not recover, use healthy leaves for cuttings.

Haworthia attenuata

A very popular and beautiful species which grows in a cluster. The variety shown here, often mistakenly labelled *Haworthia fasciata*, is *H. attenuata* var. *caespitosa*. It has white stripes on the outsides of the leaves and will grow to about 4in (10cm) tall and spread to between 8 and 12in (20–30cm). Most but not all are easy to grow and there are 100 or more names to choose from. A few of the best are *Haworthia reinwardtii, H. retusa, H. emelyae, H. comptoniana, H. limifolia, H. truncata, H. maughanii, H. bolusii, H. mirabilis, H. nigra, H. viscosa.*

Light: Do not need continuous sun but best if in sunlight 3 or 4 hours a day; or place on a brightly lit windowsill not in direct sun. In greenhouses, shade in the hottest summer months.

Temperature: Minimum 40°F (4°C). Give fresh air in summer.

Water: Water fortnightly in spring and summer, weekly in hottest months, but allow plant to dry out between waterings. Tail off in autumn, keep dry in winter. See also Introduction.

Feeding: Use high potash fertilizer 2 or 3 times in summer months.

Soil: Use good loam-based No. 2 potting compost, or soil-less compost, with 30% coarse gritty sand.

Repotting: Every spring in size larger pot. Shallow rooted species grow better in half-pots or pans. Do not water for 2 weeks.

Propagation: Whole shoots which have appeared around main plant, or individual leaves, may be removed with sharp knife (leaves can be gently eased off with fingers). Dust them with hormone rooting powder, dry for 3 days, then pot in fresh compost. Water after 3 weeks when roots have formed. Some leaves take longer. Small plants will appear later around the base of the rooted leaves.

Haworthia attenuata. Haworthias come from desert and mountain areas in South Africa and in the wild often grow under bushes, seeking a little shade from the fierce sun. This makes them ideal plants for windowsills and less sunny spots in the greenhouse, where they will receive just an hour or two of direct sun each day.

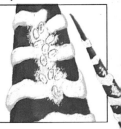

White woolly patches especially at base and tips of leaves. Mealy bug. Remove with small paintbrush dipped in methylated spirits and spray with insecticide. Repeat 2–3 times in growing season.

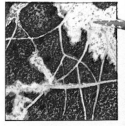

No growth though conditions correct in spring/summer. Examine roots for root mealy bug. If found, wash all soil off roots and swirl in insecticide. Leave to dry before repotting in fresh compost and clean pot. Leave dry for 2 weeks.

Plant grows slowly in spring and summer. Roots lost from overwatering or soil too heavy and compacted. Remove from pot and check roots. If rotted, pare back base to fresh tissue and dust with hormone rooting powder. Reroot in fresh, compost including at least 30% coarse gritty sand.

Green insects on flower and stem. Greenfly. Spray with pyrethrum-based insecticide and repeat every 10 days until clear.

Leaves grow long with green parts pale, white parts less bright. Too dark or, in winter, too hot and wet. Needs full light in winter and good bright light in summer with 3–4 hours full sun. Move gradually into strong light in summer to avoid scorching. In winter try to keep cooler, around 50°F (10°C), in dry soil.

what goes wrong

Leaves close up, ends shrivel. Too hot and dry. Give fresh air in summer if over 75°F (24°C) and water whenever compost dries out.

Leaves blacken and rot. Too cold and wet, too humid. In summer always allow soil to dry out between waterings. Small black spots may be signs of disease. Move out of strong sunlight and water regularly in summer. Cut out affected leaves at base with sharp knife. Do not use for propagation.

Huernia primulina

Though this plant belongs to a genus of 'Carrion flower' plants, it is suitable for growing indoors as its flowers do not have the group's characteristic smell of rotting meat. The stems make clumps to fill a 4 or 5in (10cm) pot and reach about 2in (5cm) tall in 3 or 4 years if grown well. Other good species are *Huernia zebrina*, with shining red and yellow flowers; *H. oculata*, chocolate brown and white; *H. hystrix*, greenish-yellow and brown; *H. hallii* creamy-yellow, and many others which are all easy to grow.

Huernia primulina. This is the only Huernia species with really yellow flowers, most others being mixtures of red, brown or cream. It is fly pollinated, but has little noticeable smell so it is hard to see why the flies are attracted to it.

Light: Keep in sunny position on a windowsill or in a greenhouse. Shade from full midsummer sun in greenhouse. A bright but not very sunny windowsill will be tolerated, but flowering will not be so good.

Temperature: Minimum 40°F (4°C) but 50°F (10°C) is better. Give fresh air in summer months.

Water: In spring soak in a bowl until soil wet through, then leave dry for a month. Water fortnightly in summer, weekly in hottest weather; tail off in autumn and keep dry in winter if under 55°F (13°C); if warmer, give a little water once a month. See also Introduction.

Feeding: Use high potash fertilizer 2 or 3 times during summer months.

Soil: Use good loam-based No. 2 potting compost, or soil-less compost, with 40% coarse, gritty sand.

Repotting: Every spring in size larger half-pot or pan. When old stems look unsightly, discard them when repotting, as flowers are produced on young stems from current or former year.

Propagation: Take cutting with sharp knife at natural junction of stems. Divide large clumps into clusters of 3 or 4 stems.

what goes wrong

Stems turn yellow, then black in winter. Too cold. Is plant shut behind curtains at night? Move to warmer place, above 40°F (4°C).

Stems black and shrivelled, some fall over. Too cold, wet and humid. Allow to dry out thoroughly and keep above 40°F (4°C) in winter. Pare away rot from stem. If roots black and rotted, treat and repot (see Introduction). Or, take cuttings from healthy stems.

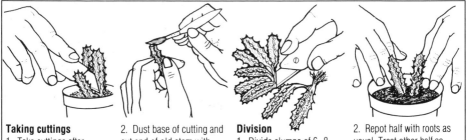

Taking cuttings
1. Take cuttings after flowering. Cut off new, outer stem where it joins old, using a sharp knife.

2. Dust base of cutting and cut end of old stem with hormone rooting powder to prevent infection and leave cutting to dry for 2 days before placing on surface of dry compost.

Division
1. Divide clumps of 6–8 stems in spring or early summer. Remove from pot and clean away any soil from lower stem. Cut through stem with sharp knife.

2. Repot half with roots as usual. Treat other half as cutting, leaving to dry for 2–3 days before rerooting.

Stems shrivel and dry. Many possible reasons. Too hot and dry in winter; too dry in spring and summer, needs feeding or root mealy bug. If soil dry in spring and summer, increase amount of water each time but allow to dry out between. In winter moisten soil monthly. If feeding and soil correct, check roots for white woolly patches. Swirl roots in insecticide, allow to dry before repotting.

Stems grow tall and pale, especially at tips. Few flowers. Too dark. Move into full light over 2 weeks. May also happen if too hot and wet in winter. Keep below 50°F (10°C) in rest period.

Brown scorch marks on stems. Sunscorch, plant moved into direct sun too quickly in stuffy place. Move out of direct light, then return gradually over 2 weeks. Keep in more airy place.

Stems shrivel, white woolly patches especially round base. Mealy bug. Remove with small paintbrush dipped in methylated spirits, and spray with contact or systemic insecticide. Repeat 2 or 3 times in growing season.

Plant collapsing or not growing, black flies around plant and soil. Sciara fly. Inspect roots and if rotted, pare back until all trace of root or larvae removed. Then treat and repot (see Introduction).

Kalanchoe blossfeldiana

This popular species, often found in florists, grows up to 12in (30cm) high with wide, fleshy green leaves. Its small red, yellow or pink flowers grow in brilliant clusters from autumn through to the spring although some can now be bought in flower at almost any time. Another good species is *Kalanchoe tomentosa* also known as the Panda plant, with velvety, silvery-green leaves with brown edges. Also available are *K. rhombopilosa* and *K. fedschtenkoi*, with lilac-purple leaves and *K. tubiflorum*, which has tiny leaf-plantlets.

Kalanchoe tomentosa, the Panda plant, has slightly furry leaves. It can be propagated easily from leaves which if gently pulled off will root on dry soil and produce several small new plants. *Kalanchoe blossfeldiana*, right, is better propagated from cuttings.

Light: Sunny conditions for best leaf colour and good flowers.

Temperature: A minimum of 45°F (7°C) but most will grow better at 50°F (10°C). Give fresh air in summer months.

Water: Fortnightly in spring and summer, weekly in hottest weather if soil dries out rapidly. Tail off in autumn and if under 45°F (7°C), keep dry in winter. If at 50°F (10°C) or over, water once a month, just enough to stop leaves from shrivelling.

Feeding: Use high potash fertilizer 2 or 3 times in the summer.

Soil: Use good loam-based No. 2 potting compost, or soil-less compost, with 20% coarse, gritty sand.

Repotting: Every spring in size larger pot.

Propagation: Take whole shoots or leaf cuttings in spring or summer. Cut shoots with a sharp knife; ease leaves off gently with as much of base as possible. Dust with hormone rooting powder, leave to dry for 3 days, then lay on fresh, dry compost. Water after 3 weeks when roots should have formed. Some Kalanchoes, (also called Bryophyllums), make little plantlets on the leaves. These may be taken off at any time and treated in the same way.

Leaves distorted as though virus infected. Usually caused by excessive use of insecticides. Use pyrethrum-based insecticides. Not fatal.

Round pieces missing from edges of leaves. Vine weevil. Sprinkle insecticide powder around base of pot and water soil with systemic insecticide to kill larvae in stem. Or slice stem from base until larvae found and reroot. (See Introduction).

Little new growth after flowering. Needs repotting or feeding. Repot each spring and feed 2–3 times in summer.

Root mealy bug
1. Check roots when repotting for root mealy bug (white woolly patches).

2. If found, wash all soil off roots under tap and swirl in insecticide diluted to maker's instructions.

3. Leave to dry for 2–3 days, then replant in fresh compost and clean pot. Do not water for 2–3 weeks.

what goes wrong

Mildewed and blackened patches on leaves. Too humid. Dust with flowers of sulphur and move to more airy place. Do not get water on leaves. If too cold and wet, stems turn black and leaves fall. Keep dry in winter unless over 50°F (10°C), when give just enough water monthly to stop leaves from shrivelling.

Stems straggly, young leaves pale or yellowish-green. Too dark. Move gradually over 2 weeks to sunny spot. If too hot and wet in winter, stems may grow tall and leaves droop. Keep around 50°F (10°C) in rest period.

White woolly patches among leaves. Mealy bug. Remove with small paintbrush dipped in methylated spirits, and spray with pyrethrum-based insecticide. Repeat 2 or 3 times in growing season.

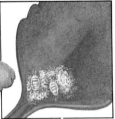

Leaves dry up and fall. Too dry or too cold. Check conditions. Best about 50°F (10°C) in winter. In summer, water when soil dries out. In winter if over 50°F (10°C) water monthly. If all conditions correct, check roots for root mealy bug (see above).

Lithops

This is a wonderful genus of South African plants, adapted to survive long, extreme droughts. They are good indoor or greenhouse plants but the watering instructions must be carefully followed. In their winter rest period new leaves grow and push through the old ones which shrivel and dry up completely. It is most important that the plants receive no water at this time. There are many species and forms with differing colours and patterning. The flowers are either yellow or white, appearing in late summer or early autumn. Good species include *L. optica* fa. *rubra*, with purple-pink stems, *L. dorotheae*, *L. otzeniana*, *L. werneri* and *L. lesliei*.

Light: Maximum sunshine is needed for these plants to ensure compact growth, good colouring and flower production.

Temperature: Low temperatures can be tolerated in the winter, but a minimum of 40°F (4°C) is safer. In summer give fresh air whenever possible.

Water: Start when the shrivelling pair of leaves are absolutely dry and crisp to the touch, usually in early summer, giving water about once a fortnight, or weekly in the really hot months after this. Stop altogether in the early winter, and do not start again until leaves have dried once more, in early summer. See also Introduction.

Feeding: Feed twice during the summer, if not repotted in spring, using high potash fertilizer. Feeding is not needed if plant has been repotted.

Soil: Use good loam-based No. 2 potting compost, or soil-less compost, with about 40% coarse, gritty sand.

Repotting: Every spring in size larger half-pot, being careful not to disturb roots.

Propagation: Usually from seed, although whole stems may be rooted in springtime.

Lithops dorotheae. This is one of the most popular 'Living stone' plants, chosen for its intricate markings. Individual heads grow to around 1in (2½cm) and are often planted with a group of differently coloured species in a shallow pan with pebbles between them to mimic their natural state. If grown in this way, make sure that the pan has drainage holes.

Leaves become elongated and lose colour. Too dark. Move into full sunlight gradually over 2 weeks. May also occur if kept too hot and wet in winter. Try to keep below 50°F (10°C) in dry soil.

Plants in greenhouse found out of pots, with triangular marks on leaf-ends. Bird damage. They often mistake them for berries. Repot and keep birds out of greenhouse.

Propagation

1. If plant has formed clump, remove single heads in spring.

2. Dust base with hormone rooting powder and leave to dry for 2–3 days.

3. Place on surface of dry compost and do not water until roots appear.

Do not pull away dead flower heads but leave them to shrivel away, only picking out by hand when they pull away easily. Pulling them out earlier may damage leaves.

what goes wrong

Two pairs of leaves actively growing at the same time on each head. Caused by watering before old leaves have shrivelled. When old leaves die, stop watering until they have dried up completely.

No flowers. Not enough light or watered at wrong time. Check conditions. If in shade, move over 2 weeks into full sunlight. Keep dry from early winter to early summer.

White woolly patches in crevices. Mealy bug. Remove with small paintbrush dipped in methylated spirits, and spray with contact or systemic insecticide. Repeat every 2–3 weeks until clear.

Plant turns black and soft. Too wet in summer or in winter too cold and humid; roots rotting. Keep above 40°F (4°C) in winter in dry atmosphere. Plant may be dead but remove from pot and inspect roots. If base rotting, pare away soft parts (see Introduction).

Leaves wither, turn brown and die. Natural. Each pair of leaves lasts only 1 year, then dies down. Do not remove old leaves until they pull away easily.

Leaves have burn marks. Moved into sun too quickly. Shade from midday sun in early summer.

Plant shows little sign of growth, and on repotting white woolly patches are found on roots. Root mealy bug. Wash all soil off roots, swirl roots in contact insecticide, and allow to dry before repotting in fresh compost and washed pot. Leave dry for two weeks before watering again.

59

Orbea variegata

This plant, also known as *Stapelia variegata*, is probably the best known of the 'Carrion flower plants', so called because its flowers smell like rotting meat. It makes large clumps which spread to fill a 5 or 6in (15cm) half-pot or pan and reach about 2½in (6cm) high in 4 or 5 years. It produces wonderful brown and creamy-yellow flowers which form 5 pointed stars 2–3in (5–7cm) across but must have a sunny position. It is easy to propagate from stems. Other good species are *Orbea ciliata*, (formerly *Diplocyatha ciliata*), with creamy-white flowers fringed with white hairs, *O. woodii* with red flowers; *O. lutea*, with a bright yellow flower. All are obtainable from specialist nurseries.

Light: A sunny position is needed to keep leaves compact and induce flowering.

Temperature: A minimum of 40°F (4°C) is needed for safety. Give fresh air in summer.

Water: Water fortnightly in spring and summer, weekly in hottest months, allow to dry out between waterings; tail off in autumn and keep dry in winter unless stems droop. Then give just enough to revive them.

Feeding: Use high potash fertilizer 2 or 3 times in summer; not necessary if repotted in spring.

Soil: Use good loam-based No. 2 potting compost, or soil-less compost, with 30% coarse, gritty sand.

Repotting: Every spring in fresh soil and size larger half-pot or pan. After 4–5 years discard older unsightly stems when repotting, retaining younger growth as this is where they flower from.

Propagation: Take cuttings of whole stems at natural junction, with sharp knife. Possible[s] from seed, but this is difficult to obtain.

Orbea variegata. Like most other carrion flower plants, this species is best kept in a sunny place outside while it is in flower as the smell from the blooms is intended to attract flies for pollination. To humans, it smells quite foul.

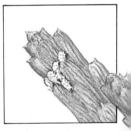

Stems shrivel, white woolly patches especially round base. Mealy bug. Remove with small paintbrush dipped in methylated spirits, and spray with contact or systemic insecticide. Repeat 2 or 3 times in growing seasons.

Stems grow long and pale, especially at tips. Few flowers. Too dark. Move into full light over 2 weeks. May also occur if too hot and wet in winter. Keep below 50°F (10°C) while resting.

Stems shrivel and do not grow in spring, conditions correct. Check roots for root mealy bug. Swirl roots in insecticide, allow to dry before repotting in fresh compost and clean pot. Leave dry for 2 weeks.

Taking cuttings
1. Cut whole new stem in late spring or early summer where it joins older ones. Outer stems are the youngest.

2. Dust cut ends with hormone rooting powder to prevent infection, leave dry for 2–3 days.

3. Then place on dry compost in small pot. Water when roots appear.

Stems turn yellow, then black in winter. Too cold. Is plant shut behind curtains at night? Move to warmer place, above 40°F (4°C).

Brown scorch marks on stems. Sunscorch, plant moved into direct sun too quickly in stuffy place. Move out of direct light, then return gradually over 2 weeks. Keep in more airy place.

Stems shrivel and dry. Many possible reasons. Too hot and dry in winter; too dry in summer, or needs feeding. If soil dry, increase amount of water each time but allow to dry out between. In winter moisten soil monthly and keep below 50°F (10°C). Feed 2–3 times in summer.

what goes wrong

Stems not growing, some black and shrivelled, some fall over. Too cold, wet and humid. Allow to dry out thoroughly and keep above 40°F (4°C) in winter. Pare away rot from stem. If roots black and rotted, treat and repot (see Introduction). Or, take cuttings from healthy stems.

Plant collapsing or not growing, black flies around plant and soil. Sciara fly. Inspect roots and if rotted, pare back until all trace of rot or larvae removed. Then treat and repot. (see Introduction.)

Pachyphytum oviferum

This popular plant is sometimes known as the 'sugared-almond plant'. The plump grey almond-shaped leaves have a delicate dusty white coating and grow in rosettes. At first it grows upright, but as the stems multiply they spread sideways to cover quite a large area: it will reach a height of 3–4in (8–10cm) and spread to between 8 and 12in (20–30cm). There are not many species in cultivation, but occasionally from specialist nurseries you can get *P. viride*, with sausage-shaped olive-green leaves, and *P. bracteosum*, with thick flattish, leaves. All are easy to grow.

Pachyphytum oviferum, the Sugared almond plant. The dusty coating on this plant's plump, oval leaves gives them their special colouring and it is important not to touch and spoil them. It flowers in spring after a winter resting period. Be careful not to get water on its leaves.

Light: A sunny position will keep the leaves of this plant blue and powdery.

Temperature: A minimum of 40°F (4°C) is needed but at 50°F (10°C) fewer leaves will fall.

Water: Start fortnightly in spring and summer, weekly in hottest weather. Tail off in autumn and if below 50°F (10°C) keep dry in winter. If above this, water monthly throughout winter. See also Introduction.

Feeding: Use high potash fertilizer 2 or 3 times in summer.

Soil: Use good loam-based No. 2 potting compost, or soil-less compost, with 30% coarse, gritty sand.

Repotting: Every spring in size larger half-pot or pan, being careful not to handle leaves, as this will damage the coating.

Propagation: Whole stems or leaves can be removed, gently with the fingers for leaves, with a sharp knife for stem cuttings. Dust cut surface with hormone rooting powder, leave dry for 3 days, then lay on dry, fresh compost. Water after 3 weeks when roots have formed.

what goes wrong

Leaves marked on edges or in patches. Damaged by contact — humans, curtains, cats? Unsightly but not fatal.

Leaves distorted as though virus infected. Caused by excessive use of insecticides, especially those based on malathion. Not usually fatal.

Round pieces missing from edges of leaves, little growth, stem swollen. Vine weevil. Sprinkle soil with insecticidal powder. Pare away stem from base until brown area in centre of stem reached, dust with hormone rooting powder and reroot (see Introduction).

Taking cuttings
Leaves will root in late spring or early summer. Choose stem well covered in leaves and remove one gently by hand. Do not use leaf from base of stem. Lay leaf flat in pot of dry compost, with base touching surface.

2. Or cut 2–3in (5–8cm) stem with good head of leaves using sharp knife; dry for 2 days, dust base of cutting and cut end of plant with hormone rooting powder to prevent infection and place cutting on dry compost. Do not water until new roots appear.

Leaves stay small and few. Needs repotting, or if soil is bone dry, more water. Soak in a bowl before watering more thoroughly each time, but always allowing to dry out between waterings.

Grows elongated in centre, leaves pale green. Too little light, move gradually over 2 weeks to a sunny spot.

Leaves look scorched. Too much sun too suddenly or lack of ventilation. Acclimatise gradually to full sun after winter and give fresh air on hot days.

Small green insects on flowers or flower-buds. Greenfly. Spray with pyrethrum-based insecticide. Repeat every 10 days until clear.

No flowers. Too dark. Keep in full light all year round.

White woolly patches between leaves, and on stem. Mealy bug. Remove with paintbrush dipped in methylated spirits, taking care to avoid damaging waxy or mealy covering to leaves, and spray with pyrethrum-based insecticide.

Leaves fall, stem becomes bare. Too cold, too dry or leaves knocked off. Check conditions. Keep around 50°F (10°C) in winter. In summer water when pot dries out. Take care when handling or watering plants as leaves are lightly attached.

Stem black and rotting, plant falls apart. Too wet. Always allow to dry out between waterings. Moisten soil monthly in winter to stop leaves falling but dry out thoroughly in between.

Little sign of growth, white woolly patches on roots. Root mealy bug. Wash all soil off roots, swirl roots in contact insecticide, and allow to dry before repotting in fresh compost and clean pot. Leave dry for 2 weeks.

Lower leaves shrivel in winter. Too hot. If keeping without water in winter, try to keep below 55°F (13°C). If hotter, water about once a month.

Pachypodium succulentum

This South African species is easy to grow. It has a large tuber, generally grown half out of the compost, as its soft tissues rot easily. From the tuber thorny branches grow up, which produce flowers in spring, followed by leaves and further flowers during the summer. The flowers vary from white, to white with a red stripe or pink with a red stripe. The plant will reach between 8 and 12in (20–30cm) tall and the same across. Other good species are *Pachypodium saundersiae* with white flowers, *P. lamerei* which is tall, *P. rosulatum*, *P. baronii*, *P. lealii*, *P. geayii* and *P. namaquanum*

Pachypodium succulentum. It is best to buy Pachypodiums as young seedlings rather than as larger plants which have already formed tubers and are more difficult to grow indoors. Remember to spray the stems occasionally during the winter rest period, to prevent the ends from shrivelling.

Light: All Pachypodiums need full sun.
Temperature: Minimum 55°F (13°C) although South African species will tolerate down to 40°F (4°C) in winter if dry.
Water: Start watering fortnightly when signs of growth appear, usually in late spring. Allow soil to dry out between waterings. Water weekly in hottest weather, tail off to fortnightly in autumn and withhold from early winter, when the leaves will go brown and fall. Do not water again until leaves begin to reappear. Spray tips of shoots monthly in winter to prevent them from drying. See also Introduction.
Feeding: Use high potash fertilizer 2 or 3 times in summer months.
Soil: Loam-based No. 2 or soil-less compost, with 40% coarse, gritty sand.
Repotting: Avoid damage to roots when repotting each spring into a size larger pot. After 6in (15cm) pot is reached do not repot for 2 or 3 years, but feed regularly.
Propagation: Best from seed, from specialist seed nurseries. Seedlings grow quickly and the taller-growing types will reach about 8in (20cm) in 3 or 4 years.

Tips of shoots die back, becoming brown and hardened; shoots break out from well below tips in spring. Spraying tips in winter will stop this excessive drying up. Remove damaged tips when absolutely dry with sharp scissors or secateurs. Do not cut into healthy stems.

White woolly patches among leaves. Mealy bug. Remove with small paintbrush dipped in methylated spirits, and spray with insecticide. Repeat 2 or 3 times in growing season.

what goes wrong

Leaves marked with brown or white patches. Brown is scorch from sudden hot sun in stuffy place. White is from insecticides or hard water spray. Remove with rainwater and small paintbrush.

Flowers shrivel quickly. Too hot and dry. Check soil regularly and water when it dries out in summer. Do not expose to hot sun after cloudy weather: move gradually into full light.

Leaves turn pale green or yellow-green, no flowers. Too dark. Bring gradually into full sun over 2 weeks.

Little sign of new growth in spring. Needs feeding or repotting or root mealy bug. Check roots and if white woolly patches found, wash soil away, swirl roots in insecticide and allow to dry before repotting in fresh compost and clean pot. Leave dry for 2 weeks.

Leaves blacken and fall, stem ends soft, tuber soft. Too cold and wet. Move to warmer place, at least 55°F (13°C) and allow to dry out before watering again. Always keep dry in winter even in normal room temperatures. Pare away rotting tissue and dust with fungicide. If conditions correct, check roots for sciara fly or vine weevil maggots (see Introduction). If rot is severe, plant will die.

Leaves turn paler, shrivel and fall. In summer, too hot and dry or too wet. Check conditions. If dry, soak in bowl of water for ½ an hour, then drain. If soil dark and soggy, leave to dry out completely before watering again. If new leaves do not grow but stem firm, repot in fresh, dry compost. Do not water again for 2 weeks. Leaves fall in autumn/winter, and grow again in spring.

When received plant has soft patches in bulbous stem or roots, and on cutting, has orange patches in the tissue. Damage to roots has allowed orange rot to get a hold. Pare away narrow slices with sharp clean knife until no sign of orange is visible. Dust with hormone rooting powder containing fungicide; allow to dry thoroughly before rerooting in dry compost.

65

Pelargonium rhodantha

This is one of the many species used to produce the well-known garden Pelargonium. They vary from plants with a stem similar to that of the garden hybrids to thick, woody stems like gnarled bonsai trees. They have a dormant period when the leaves fall, and often produce flowers as they start to grow, with the first leaves of the new season. They will reach a height of 8–12in (20–30cm) and spread over 6–8in (15–20cm). Specialist nurseries carry them from time to time, often as dried up twigs which, when kept damp for a few weeks, produce leaves. Other species include *Pelargonium cortusifolium*, *P. crassicaule*, *P. alternans*, and *P. klinghardtense*. The closely related Sarcocaulon genus is regarded by some authorities as the same, and two of the best Sarcocaulons are *S. burmannii* and *S. multifidum*.

Pelargonium rhodantha. Succulent pelargoniums are stem succulents. The leaves drop in winter but if the stem is thick and woody, they are less likely to dry out completely. The dainty flowers often appear with the first new leaves at the beginning of the spring growing season.

Light: Full sun all year round.

Temperature: A minimum of 40°F (4°C) is necessary for safety in the winter, but 45°F (7°C) is better.

Water: Start in early spring, with a good soaking to induce leaves or flowers to emerge. Then water fortnightly, allowing to dry out between waterings, weekly in hot weather. Tail off in autumn and keep dry from early winter. See also Introduction.

Feeding: Use high potash fertilizer 2 or 3 times in the summer.

Soil: Loam-based No. 2 or soil-less compost, with 30% gritty sand.

Repotting: Every spring in size larger pot, if it has outgrown its old pot. If not, repot in fresh compost in same size pot.

Propagation: From cuttings in spring.

White woolly patches among leaves. Mealy bug. Remove with paintbrush dipped in methylated spirits and spray with insecticide. Repeat 2 or 3 times in spring and summer.

Tiny white flies fly up when plant touched. Whitefly. Spray with insecticide that specifies pest. Repeat after 2 weeks, then 4 weeks later.

Leaves turn light brown, with fine webs. Red spider mite. Spray with insecticide every 10 days until clear. Then spray every 2 months to prevent attack. Darker burn marks may be sunscorch: plant moved too suddenly into bright light.

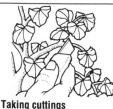

Taking cuttings
1. Take cuttings 2–3in (5–8cm) long in spring or early summer.

2. Remove lowest leaf if close to cut end and dust end of cutting and end of cut stem with hormone rooting powder.

3. Plant in dry compost and do not water for 2–3 weeks or until new roots appear.

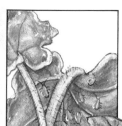

Green insects on flowers, buds or back of leaves. Greenfly. Spray every 10 days with pyrethrum-based insecticide until clear.

Leaf stalks long, leaves pale whitish-green. Too dark. Move to sunny position over 2 weeks. If leaves remain on but are pale in winter, too hot and wet. Allow to dry out in winter and try to keep around 50°F (10°C) during rest period.

Plant fails to grow. Needs repotting or feeding or, if conditions correct, check roots for root mealy bug. If found, wash all soil off roots, swirl in contact insecticide and allow to dry before repotting in fresh compost and clean pot. Leave dry for 2 weeks.

what goes wrong

Leaves turn brown, dry up and fall. Too dry in spring and summer, in autumn and winter natural as plant starts resting period. In growing period soak in bowl of water, then water more generously each time: allow to dry out between waterings. If stem tips shrivel in winter, spray monthly.

Leaves black and fall, stem ends black and soft. Too cold and wet. Move to warmer place and allow to dry out. Pare away blackened stem and dust with fungicide. Keep dry in winter and give less water each time in summer.

Pleiospilos

This is another South African plant that mimics stones. It is similar to Lithops but the plant bodies look like pieces of broken, weathered grey rock instead of smooth pebbles and are about 2in (5cm) high and 2½in (6cm) across. *Pleiospilos hilmari* is more attractively coloured than most species, with purple tinges overlaying a minutely spotted surface. It produces its bright yellow flowers freely in late summer. The main causes of problems for growing this plant are: not enough light, and water at the wrong time, which causes the body to split, or even to rot completely. Other species are *Pleiospilos bolusii*, grey and angular, *P. nelii*, rounded, grey-brown, *P. willowmorensis*, with longer leaves than most, *P. prismaticus* and *P. simulans*, and others.

Pleiospilos hilmari. These small stone-like plants, known as Living rocks, are often hard to distinguish from the pebbles around them. They sometimes grow in clumps but single, 2 or 3-headed plants are most common. The bright yellow flowers appear from between the thick leaves in late summer.

Light: A sunny windowsill is needed for best results, although there is a danger of scorching in spring, especially if a period of cloudy weather is followed by some days of strong sunshine.

Temperature: Minimum 40°F (4°C) for safety. Give fresh air in summer.

Water: Do not water until early summer, then only once every two or three weeks, making sure the soil has dried out between waterings. Tail off in late autumn; do not water in winter and spring.

Feeding: Only if not repotted for 3 years; use high potash fertilizer, only twice during summer.

Soil: Use good loam-based No. 2 potting compost, or soil-less compost, with 50% coarse, gritty sand added.

Repotting: Every year when young; after 3 years, repot every other year. Leave dry for 2 weeks after repotting in late spring.

Propagation: Old clumps may be increased from cuttings, but best from seed.

Two pairs of leaves actively growing at the same time on each head. Caused by watering before old leaves have shrivelled. When old leaves die, stop watering until they have dried up completely.

what goes wrong

Plant shows little sign of growth, and on repotting white woolly patches are found on roots. Root mealy bug. Wash all soil off roots, swirl roots in contact insecticide, and allow to dry before repotting in fresh compost and washed pot. Leave dry for two weeks before watering again.

2. Water from base with fungicide diluted as for 'damping off' of seedlings, until surface is damp. Place tray or pot in polythene bag with ends folded underneath to seal in moisture. Leave in light (not direct sun) a 70°F (21°C).

Leaves become elongated and lose colour. Too dark. Move into full sunlight gradually over 2 weeks. May also occur if too hot and wet in winter.

No flowers. Not enough light or watered at wrong time. Check conditions. If in shade, move over 2 weeks into full sunlight. Keep dry from early winter to early summer.

White woolly patches in crevices and between new and old leaves. Mealy bug. Remove with small paintbrush dipped in methylated spirits, and spray with contact or systemic insecticide. Repeat every 2–3 weeks until clear.

Leaves split and crack open. Water at wrong time of year or overwatering. Allow to dry out then give less water each time and keep dry in winter. Not fatal but will not heal up.

Plant marked. Either mealy covering damaged by handling or sunscorch. Shade from midday sun in early summer. Give fresh air in hot weather.

Plant turns black and soft. Too wet in summer or winter or too cold and humid; roots rotting. Keep above 40°F (4°C) in winter in dry atmosphere. Treat roots (see Introduction).

Leaves wither, turn brown and die. Natural. Each pair of leaves lasts only 1 year, then dies down. Do not remove old leaves until they pull away easily.

69

Portulacaria afra

The only species of this South African genus comes in either a green-leaved form, or the more attractive, variegated, yellow and green leaved form shown here. It is slow-growing, making a low 'bonsai' type of plant some 10in (25cm) across and 5–6in (12–15cm) tall in 5 to 10 years. The flowers, which are rare in cultivation, are similar to groundsel, yellow and daisy-like. This beautiful succulent plant is grown for its foliage and is an ideal subject for a half-pot or bowl, or even a hanging basket.

Light: A sunny position is needed for best results, but provided it gets an hour or two of sunshine each day it will grow well.

Temperature: A minimum of 40°F (4°C) is needed. Give fresh air in summer.

Water: Start watering in spring. Water fortnightly in spring and summer, weekly in hottest weather. Tail off in autumn, giving none in winter. See also Introduction.

Feeding: Use high potash fertilizer 2 or 3 times in summer.

Soil: Use good loam-based No. 2 potting compost, or soil-less compost, with 30% coarse, gritty sand.

Repotting: Every spring when young, leave 2 or 3 years when stems reach about 9in (22cm). Do not water for 2 weeks after repotting. Be careful not to knock off leaves when repotting as they are fragile.

Propagation: Lengths of stem about 2in (5cm) can be cut off in spring and summer, dusted with hormone rooting powder, left to dry for a few days, then rooted in dry compost. Water after about 3 weeks when roots start to appear. Also possible from seed, if obtainable, but it is rarely available. The tiny seedlings should not be allowed to dry out for the first 6 months.

Portulacaria afra variegata looks like a miniature Jade tree. It is a slow grower, taking some 5 years to grow into a 5in (13cm) pan or half-pot but looks attractive both in a normal pot and in a hanging basket. Flowers are rare when grown indoors.

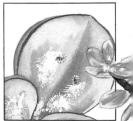

White woolly patches among leaves. Mealy bug. Remove with small paintbrush dipped in methylated spirits, and spray with contact or systemic insecticide. Repeat every 2 weeks until clear.

Bottom leaves fall, little new growth. Needs repotting or feeding. Repot every spring in fresh compost and feed 2 or 3 times a year with high potash plant food. If conditions correct, inspect roots for root mealy bug (white woolly patches on roots). Wash all soil off roots, swirl in contact insecticide, and allow to dry before repotting in fresh compost and washed pot. Leave dry for two weeks.

Propagation

1. When taking cuttings in spring or summer, cut stem with sharp knife just below a leaf. Dust both cut ends with hormone rooting powder to prevent infection.

2. If growing from seed, water half pot or tray regularly by standing in outer container of water until surface is damp.

Leaves turn black and fall, stem ends turn black and go soft, roots rot. Too cold and probably too wet. Keep above 40°F (4°C). Pare off blackened part of stem and dust with hormone rooting powder containing fungicide. If roots rotted, see Introduction.

what goes wrong

Stems grow long with few, pale leaves. Too dark or, in winter, too hot and wet. Keep in full light all year round but if in shade, move into sunlight gradually over 2 weeks to prevent scorching. In winter keep dry, below 50°F (10°C) if possible.

Leaves become crisp and brown, then fall. Too dry for too long. If summer or spring soak in bowl of water for half an hour, then drain and allow almost to dry out before watering again. Water more regularly. In winter water once a month to prevent soil drying out completely.

Brown patches on leaves. Sun scorch. Move to more airy place and shade from hot sun for 2 weeks. Then move gradually back, over period of 2 weeks.

Round pieces missing from leaf edges, stem swollen; little new growth. Vine weevil. Sprinkle insecticide powder around base of pot and water soil with systemic insecticide to kill larvae in stem. Or slice stem from base until larvae found and reroot.

Sedum morganianum

This is one of a vast genus of succulent plants, widespread in both tropical and temperate climates. *Sedum morganianum* from Mexico is one of the most attractive of the tender species which all have fleshy stems or leaves. It needs to be kept indoors or in a greenhouse, and is an ideal subject for a hanging basket. It does better out of the full glare of the sun in summer, but must have a good light position all year. The stems will grow up to about 3ft (1m) and cover a base area of about 8in (20cm). Other good species, not for hanging baskets, are *Sedum rubrotinctum*, especially 'Aurora', *S. hintonii*, and *S. furfuraceum*.

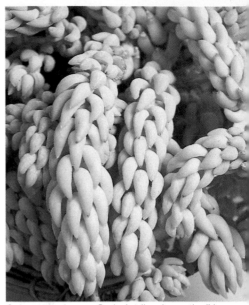

Sedum morganianum or Donkey's tail, makes a splendid hanging pot plant. Be careful not to allow it to dry out completely in winter or the leaves will become crisp and fall leaving unsightly areas of bare stem. Pink flowers appear from the ends of the stems but only on very large mature plants: its leaves are its main indoor attraction.

Light: To bring out the best colouring full sunshine is needed at all times.

Temperature: Many species will take temperatures near freezing, but are better kept at a minimum 40°F (4°C) in winter. Give fresh air in summer.

Water: Spray heavily monthly in winter, or give just enough water to keep the soil from drying out completely once a month or every six weeks. Water fortnightly in spring and summer, weekly in hottest weather. Tail off in autumn. See also Introduction.

Feeding: Not needed if repotted each year. Use high potash fertilizer if not repotted, not more than twice in summer.

Soil: Use good loam-based No. 1 potting compost, or soil-less compost, with 30% coarse, gritty sand.

Repotting: Every spring until they are in 5in (13cm) half pot or pan, then every other year. Always use shallow pots as the roots are short. Do not water for 2 weeks after repotting.

Propagation: By whole stem cuttings or leaf-cuttings.

Taking cuttings

1. Cut stem 2in (5cm) from end, between leaves in late spring or early summer. Dust cut ends with hormone rooting powder to prevent infection, leave to dry for 2 days, then place cutting on dry compost. Do not water until roots appear.

2. Or, ease off leaf from healthy stem with fingers and lay flat on dry compost, with base touching surface. Do not water until roots form and do not remove old leaf until quite dried out.

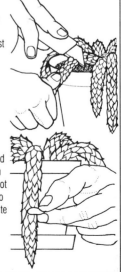

what goes wrong

No growth, leaves fall leaving tuft at stem end. If lower stem soft or blackened, overwatered. Allow to dry out well before watering again and pare away blackened stem (see Introduction). In winter water only once a month. If conditions correct and stem firm, check roots for root mealy bug.

No flowers. Too dark. Move to full sun over 2 weeks. Needs sunshine all year round.

Stems short, have not grown in spring and summer. Compost unsuitable or has not been repotted or fed. Repot following spring in fresh compost or feed twice during summer. Do not feed in winter.

New leaves small, little new growth in spring. Needs repotting in half-pot or pan with fresh compost. Take care not to damage the leaves

when repotting and choose pot only one size larger each time.

Leaves next to glass light brown and shrivelled. Sunscorched, probably after cloudy period. Shade for 2 weeks, then move back gradually to full sun. In hot summer weather, shade from midday sun.

Long gaps of bare stem between leaves. Too dark. Move to sunny place over 2 weeks.

White woolly patches among leaves. Mealy bug. Remove with small paintbrush dipped in methylated spirits and spray with insecticide. Repeat 2–3 times in spring and summer.

Hanging baskets

Leaves shrivel and fall. Too dry. Soak in bowl of water for ½ hour, then drain and give more water each time soil dries out. In winter moisten soil monthly, to keep leaves plump.

Leaves wrinkle, turn black and fall; stem ends black and soft. Too cold and wet or too humid. Move to warmer place, around 50°F (10°C) in winter and allow to dry out if soil wet. Pare away blackened area and dust with fungicide.

Plants in hanging baskets dry out more quickly than those in standing containers. Check compost regularly and water when pot dries out in summer. In winter, spray monthly, especially if over 50°F (10°C) to prevent leaves from falling.

73

Senecio haworthii

Several members of this genus are classed as succulents, and *Senecio haworthii*, sometimes labelled *Kleinia tomentosa*, is one of the most attractive. It has stark white leaves made from a dense covering of clinging, spiderweb-like wool. A very sunny spot is needed to produce the yellow flowers in cultivation, as this plant comes from South Africa and is well adapted to withstand the strong sunlight it receives there. It will grow to between 10 and 12in (25–30cm) tall and 4–6in (10–15cm) across. Other species worth looking out for are: *Senecio medley-woodii*, with flat woolly leaves and *S. rowleyanus*, with hanging stems and pea-like leaves.

Light: Full sunshine is needed to bring out the best colouring.

Temperature: A minimum of 45°F (7°C) is needed. Give fresh air in summer.

Water: Water fortnightly in spring and summer, but allow to dry out between waterings. Water weekly in the hottest weather. Tail off in autumn and in winter give just enough to keep soil from becoming dust dry – about once a month. See also Introduction.

Feeding: Use high potash fertilizer 3 or 4 times in the summer.

Soil: Use good loam-based No. 2 compost, or soil-less compost, with 30% coarse, gritty sand.

Repotting: Every spring in size larger pot until 5 or 6in (15cm) is reached. Then gently shake soil off roots and repot in same size clean pot with fresh soil. Do not water for 2 weeks after repotting.

Propagation: Cuttings may be taken in spring and summer, dried off for 2 or 3 days after dusting lightly with hormone rooting powder and placed in fresh, dry compost.

Senecio haworthii. A well grown plant will have leaves all the way up the stem. It needs careful watering: if it is too dry, the lower leaves will fall, if too wet the roots will rot. Make sure it is planted in a compost containing plenty of grit so that excess water can drain off quickly.

Leaves wrinkle and fall, leaving topknot on each stem. Stems shrivel. Too dry or too hot in winter. In winter water once a month if leaves start to wrinkle and fall and keep around 50°F (10°C). In spring and summer give more water each time, but allow to dry out between waterings. Give fresh air in hot weather.

what goes wrong

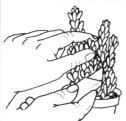

Taking cuttings

1. In spring or early summer, cut off stem about 2in (5cm) from tip, between leaves.

2. If no bare stem shows, remove lowest leaf. Dust cut ends with hormone rooting powder to prevent infection. Leave to dry for 2 days.

3. Place on surface of dry compost and do not water until roots appear in 2–3 weeks time.

Little new growth, white woolly patches on roots. Root mealy bug. Wash all soil off roots, swirl roots in contact insecticide and allow to dry before repotting in fresh compost and clean pot. Leave dry for 2 weeks.

Long spaces between leaves, little white covering on new ones. Too dark. Move into full sun over 2 weeks.

Leaves turn black and fall, stem black and soft. Too cold and wet or too humid. Keep warmer, above 45°F (7°C) in winter. Pare off blackened part of stem and dust with fungicide. In winter give just enough water once a month to prevent leaf fall and in summer always allow to dry out between waterings.

Leaves shrivel and have brown scorch marks. Too hot and stuffy, sunscorched. Give fresh air in summer and move out of bright sunlight. Reintroduce gradually over 2 weeks.

White woolly patches among leaves. Mealy bug. Remove with small paintbrush dipped in methylated spirits and spray with contact or systemic insecticides. Repeat 2 or 3 times in growing season.

Leaves on lower stem fall, little new growth. Needs repotting urgently. Repot with fresh compost each spring.

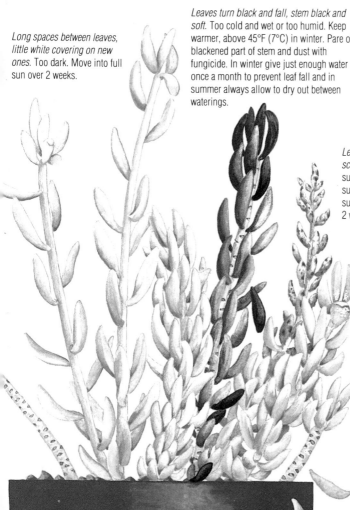

75

Stapelia pulvinata

Another of the 'carrion-flowered' succulents, so-called because the flowers look and smell like rotting meat. *Stapelia pulvinata* produces large, hairy, starfish shaped red to reddish-brown flowers on its fine, velvety stems. Their unpleasant smell attracts flies and you may find that fly eggs have been laid on the plant. The hatching maggots have nothing to feed on and soon die. If the flowers have been pollinated, long seed-pods like cattle-horns form in pairs, splitting eventually to let out the thistle-like seeds. Many species are available.

Stapelia pulvinata. This carrion-flower's hairy, red or reddish-brown flowers grow on velvety stems at the base of the plant. The plant itself will grow quite large with stems up to 6in (15cm) tall and it is important to repot each year into a larger container to allow for fresh growth, as flowers develop on the newer stems.

Light: For good flowers these plants need a sunny position. A little shading is needed in the hottest weather (over 90°F, 32°C) if in a greenhouse.

Temperature: A minimum of 40°F (4°C). Give fresh air if over 80°F (27°C).

Stems become elongated, pale green, especially at tips; no flowers produced. Too little light. Move gradually to lighter position over 2 weeks.

Water: Fortnightly in spring and summer, weekly in hottest weather, but always make sure soil has dried out. Tail off in autumn, keep dry in winter unless stems droop. Then give just enough to revive them – once a month should be sufficient. Incorporate systemic fungicide 2 or 3 times in spring and summer. See also Introduction.

Feeding: Use high potash fertilizer 3 or 4 times in spring and summer.

Soil: Use good loam-based No. 2 potting compost, or soil-less compost, with 40% coarse, gritty sand.

All stems shrivel in summer though conditions and care correct. Remove from pot and look for white woolly patches among roots (root mealy bug). If found, wash soil off roots, swirl in insecticide diluted in water and leave to dry before repotting in clean pot and fresh compost.

Repotting: Every spring in size larger half-pot or pan until in 6 or 8in (15cm) size. Then best to repropagate from shoots. Do not water for 2 weeks after repotting.

Propagation: Cut young shoots 2–3in long and leave to dry for 2 days. Dust base with hormone rooting powder containing fungicide, then place on dry compost until roots begin to form (2–3 weeks). Start watering.

Stems do not grow in spring and summer. Needs repotting or feeding. Repot every spring into size larger pot with fresh compost and feed 3–4 times in spring and summer.

what goes wrong

Taking cuttings
Use young shoots 2–3in (5–8cm) long for cuttings in spring or summer. Cut as close to base as possible, dust both cut ends with hormone rooting powder to prevent infection, then leave dry for 2 days. Then place cutting in dry compost and do not water until new roots appear.

Stems turn black and soft. Overwatering and too cold. Check roots and if rotted separate healthy stems. Pare away roots until healthy tissue reached. Dust with hormone rooting powder and use as cuttings. Keep dry, above 40°F (4°C) in winter.

Stems turn brown and shrivelled in summer. Too dry. Plunge pot into bowl of water for half an hour, then drain. Water when pot dries out in spring and summer, so test compost regularly in hot weather. Stems may turn bronze if suddenly exposed to direct hot sun and may scorch if in stuffy place. Give fresh air when temperature over 80°F (27°C).

In winter months stem goes first yellow, then black. Too cold; plant may have been shut behind curtains. Move to warmer position, over 40°F (4°C) or bring inside before drawing curtains at night.

White woolly patches on stems, especially around base. Mealy bug. Remove with small paintbrush dipped in methylated spirits. Remove plant from pot and discard soil, which may contain eggs of pest. Dip stems in insecticide, leave for 3 days to dry before repotting in fresh soil and clean pot.

Tips of stems die back in winter. Too hot. Try to keep in cool room, below 50°F (10°C) in dry resting period. But keep in good light.

Tiny black flies around plant and on surface of soil: plant may be collapsing. Sciara or mushroom fly. Roots have probably rotted, so lift stems and pare from the base until no trace of larvae or brown rot is seen. Dust with hormone rooting powder and leave to dry for 3 days, before treating as cuttings.

77

Testudinaria elephantipes

This intriguing plant has a large, swollen corky stem shaped rather like an elephant's foot. It generally lies dormant between spring and late summer or autumn, then sends up a vine with heart-shaped leaves and tiny flowers. In mature plants the vine may grow up to 6ft (2m) long before dying down again in late winter. Regular watering and feeding while the vine is growing increases the size of the plant's corky stem – its main attraction. One or two other species are occasionally seen.

Light: Full sun best, but will also grow well on a windowsill out of direct sun – but not shaded from the light.

Temperature: A minimum of 40°F (4°C) for safety, although if root is dry it will take temperatures to nearly freezing.

Water: Start when there are signs of growth, usually but not always in late autumn. Water every 2 weeks while vine is growing and producing leaves, but always allow to dry out between waterings. Test soil regularly as in cloudy weather it stays damp for longer. When leaves turn brown and fall in spring, water once more to make sure it is not just too dry, then stop until growth begins again. See also Introduction.

Feeding: use high potash fertilizer 2 or 3 times when vine is growing.

Soil: Use good loam-based No. 2 potting compost, or soil-less compost, with 30% coarse, gritty sand.

Repotting: Every year in early years until 6in (15cm) pot is reached, then every 2 or 3 years will do. Do not water for 2 weeks after repotting.

Propagation: Only possible from seed, which is often available from specialist nurseries.

Testudinaria elephantipes, Elephant foot plant. In late summer or autumn, stems shoot up from the corky tuber and may grow up to 8 or 10ft (3m) in a season. The stems need some sort of support, either on a cord suspended from above or trained around a curved bamboo cane.

Leaves brown and fall. In autumn and winter too dry or too wet. Check conditions. If dry, increase amount of water each time, but allow to dry out thoroughly between waterings. If soil soggy, inspect roots and cut away rot In spring leaves fall naturally but check compost and continue watering in case caused by dryness. If leaves continue to fall, stop watering until new shoots appear in autumn.

Stem soft and squashy, no leaves grow in autumn/winter. Overwatered or watered at the wrong time; or too cold. The plant will have died. Check watering instructions carefully before growing a new plant. Always allow to dry out between waterings.

Leaves scorched, stems die back. Too sudden exposure to strong sun and too stuffy an atmosphere. Move out of strong sunlight · and gradually move back over 2 weeks. Keep in more airy place. Remove unsightly leaves and stem with sharp scissors or secateurs.

Leaves have brown or white marks. Caused by insecticide spray or hard water. Not fatal.

Vine stem has long spaces between pale leaves and does not grow well. Too dark. Move gradually over 2 weeks into full sunlight.

Removing the stem
When stem begins to turn yellow and die in late winter, stop watering and allow compost to dry out. Cut stems near corky base with secateurs or sharp scissors.

Green insects on leaves and vine stems. Greenfly. Spray with pyrethrum-based insecticide, and repeat every 10 days until clear.

what goes wrong

Vine stem grows quickly and needs support. Insert cane or plant trellis in pot or provide hanging cord. Tie stem loosely to support, making sure knot is against cane, not plant stem.

Corky stem does not enlarge. Needs feeding. Feed 2–3 times in autumn and winter, when new leaves growing.

Buying your succulent

Succulent plants are often seen offered for sale in garden centres, general nurseries and florists together with cacti. Sometimes they are of good quality and well cared for, but more often, unfortunately, they have been wrongly treated and are a bedraggled, damaged, starved-of-light collection. Many will be unlabelled and it is difficult to find out from a general plant supplier how to look after them.

Specialist nurseries are best for unusual succulents and they can normally be bought either by personal visit, or, perhaps more conveniently, by post as they travel well. Advertisements in gardening journals, particularly those of the cactus & succulent societies, will lead you to the best sources.

It is important before buying to consider the conditions you can provide for these plants. If you are a beginner, choose plants that are simple to grow. Do not be tempted to buy the more difficult ones until you have gained some experience, and do not buy too many from the same source, especially by post, until you have made sure the quality is good.

Look carefully at plants you intend to buy, and where they are being kept. If they are showing signs of stretched growth at the tips and are in a poorly lit place, they may already be severely weakened. Or if they have blackened leaves and have been kept outside in very cold weather they may already be fatally damaged.

Bright colouring, with reddish tinges to the leaves of some plants, shows that they have been kept in a light position.

The best time to buy is in the late spring or summer months when most of the plants will be in active growth and will show it. If you grow your own plants well you will soon learn what a healthy plant looks like and know what to look for. Lastly, make sure your plant has a label or ask the nurseryman if he knows at least what genus it belongs to, so that you can look up its care instructions. When you get it home, inspect it for pests (the roots as well), repot it into your own compost, and leave it dry for 2 weeks. If possible keep it away from your other plants until you have ascertained that it is pest free. Do the same with plants sent by post. These usually arrive without pots, so get some ready before they arrive.

The Cactus and Succulent Society of America can be contacted at 2631 Fairgreen Avenue, Arcadia, California 91006

Acknowledgements

Colour artwork by Bob Bampton/The Garden Studio (pp. 15, 21, 23, 33, 35, 37, 39, 49, 55, 57, 59, 63). Paul Wrigley/The Garden Studio (pp. 17, 19, 25, 27, 41, 45, 47, 53, 73, 75, 77). Steve Kirk (pp. 29, 65, 71, 78). Jane Pickering/Linden Artists Ltd (pp. 43, 51, 67). Josephine Martin/The Garden Studio (pp. 31, 61, 69)
Line artwork by Marion Neville, Patricia Newton, Norman Bancroft-Hunt
Photographs by David Cockroft, Bill Weightman
Additional photographs supplied by Gordon Rowley and The Harry Smith Horticultural Photographic Collection. Additional plants supplied by The Cactus Place, Upminster.
Designed by Marion Neville
Typeset by Oxford Publishing Services